The Secret of Secrets

١٣
٢٦

The Secret of Secrets

by

ḤAḌRAT ʿABDUL-QĀḌIR AL-JĪLĀNĪ

(May Allah sanctify his secret)

interpreted by

Shaykh Tosun Bayrak al-Jerrahi al-Halveti

THE ISLAMIC TEXTS SOCIETY

This edition published 1992 by
The Islamic Texts Society
Miller's House
Kings Mill Lane
Great Shelford
Cambridge CB22 5EN
United Kingdom
www.its.org.uk

British Library Cataloguing-in-Publication Data.
A catalogue record for this book is available from the British Library.

ISBN: 978 0946621 29 3 paper

Reprint 1994, 1997, 1999, 2002, 2006, 2008, 2010, 2011, 2012, 2014, 2016, 2018, 2019, 2020, 2021, 2025

Printed and bound in the UK by SRP, Exeter EX2 7LW.

Contents

Foreword/IX

Translator's Introduction/XIII

An Address to the Reader/XLVII

The Secret of Secrets

Introduction/3

CHAPTER ONE
Man's Return Home to the Original Source/13

CHAPTER TWO
The Descent of Man to the Lowest of the Low/18

CHAPTER THREE
The Places of the Souls within the Body/20

CHAPTER FOUR
On Knowledge/26

CHAPTER FIVE
On Repentance and On Teaching by the Word/31

CHAPTER SIX
On Islamic Mysticism and the Sufis/40

CHAPTER SEVEN
On Remembrance/45

CHAPTER EIGHT
The Necessary Conditions for Remembrance/48

CHAPTER NINE
On the Vision of Allah: Arriving at the Level of Seeing the Manifestation of the Divine Essence/51

CHAPTER TEN
The Veils of Light and Darkness/55

CHAPTER ELEVEN
The Joy of Being Good and the Misery of the Rebel/58

CHAPTER TWELVE
The Dervishes/65

CHAPTER THIRTEEN
On the Purification of the Self/71

CHAPTER FOURTEEN
On the Meaning of Ritual Worship and Inner Worship/73

CHAPTER FIFTEEN
On the Purification of the Perfect Man, who has Isolated Himself from, and Stripped Himself of, All Worldly Concerns/76

CHAPTER SIXTEEN
On Charity/79

CHAPTER SEVENTEEN
On Fasting Prescribed by the Religion and On Spiritual Fasting/82

CHAPTER EIGHTEEN
On the Pilgrimage to Makka and the Inner Pilgrimage to the Essence of the Heart/84

CHAPTER NINETEEN
On Witnessing Divine Truth through the State of Peace Coming from Abandonment of the Worldly and through Ecstasy/89

CHAPTER TWENTY
On Withdrawing from the World into Seclusion and On Solitude/93

CHAPTER TWENTY-ONE
Prayers and Recitations Pertaining to the Path of Seclusion/98

CHAPTER TWENTY-TWO
On Dreams/108

CHAPTER TWENTY-THREE
On the Followers of the Mystical Path/116

CHAPTER TWENTY-FOUR
Afterword/120

Foreword

And when your Lord said to the angels, I am going to place in the earth a viceregent... and He taught Adam all the names... And when We said to the angels: Make obeisance to Adam, they did obeisance... (Sūra Baqara, 30, 31, 34)

When Allah created Adam عليه السلام He made him superior to the angels by endowing him with knowledge of the essence of the entire creation. The Names taught to Adam عليه السلام were Allah's attributes and qualities. Each special divine quality involved in the creation of an object is manifested in that object. When Adam received the Names, all these qualities were implanted within his being, and through them he understood the whole universe. Allah then set him within the world to serve as His viceregent.

The descendants of Adam عليه السلام inherit this endowment as a potential capacity, varying in nature from individual to individual. As people's gifts differ, so also do their ranges of accountability to Allah and the particular forms their viceregency must assume. This is so even at the highest levels, as is illustrated in Sūra Kahf (60–82) by the different roles played by Moses عليه السلام, the embodiment of moral righteousness, and Khiḍr عليه السلام, the demonstrator of mystical insight. But the supreme viceregency, universal and comprehensive, was manifested in the Prophet Muḥammad صلى الله عليه وسلم.

It is necessary for each individual to understand the nature and range of his potential gift. Only then can he know his actual relationship with the universe and his Creator and fulfil his trust, the function of viceregency that he has accepted. And only then can he realize the true meaning and significance of the divine ordinances brought by the Holy Prophet ﷺ.

Without this understanding, there is a danger that the teachings of religion may remain only an external dress, to be adhered to outwardly but not activated inwardly. When this happens, the practice of religion turns into a rule of customs and conventions, and the presence of Allah within the heart is not realized.

It is true that Paradise is promised to those who simply and sincerely follow Allah's commandments and the Prophet's instructions, but *Those who are believers among you, and the learned, Allah will increase their rank* (Sūra Mujādila, 11), and, *Are those who are learned equal to those who are ignorant?* (Sūra Zumar, 9).

Sūra Wāqi'a shows that the ultimate division of humanity will be into three categories and not just two—people bound for Hell, people bound for Paradise, and, out of the latter, people *closest to Allah* (Sūra Wāqi'a, 7–11).

In the final reckoning, those who have striven and have been blessed with knowledge of themselves and their Lord will have a higher rank. For this knowledge increases one's love for Allah and the Prophet ﷺ, and the more one loves, the closer one can draw. With such knowledge, one understands that the practices of religion are the form of wisdom, and that by accepting the form one realizes the substance. The ways and means of realizing the substance within the form make up what is called Sufism.

Sirr al-asrār gives, within its brief compass, the very essence of Sufism. Though many Sufis had written before him, it was Ḥaḍrat ʿAbdul-Qādir al-Jīlānī, may Allah be pleased with him, who most clearly defined the path and explained the terms which, since then, have become accepted usage. In this book he gives a Sufi explanation of the fundamental duties of Islam—prayer, fasting, almsgiving and pilgrimage. It thus forms a bridge between his two more famous works, *Ghunyat al-ṭālibīn*, 'Wealth for Seekers', which is meant to inspire men and women to be good practicing Muslims, and *Futūḥ al-ghayb*, 'Revelation of the Unseen', a late collection of lectures on mystical topics. Unless one passes through *Sirr al-asrār*, one may not be able to appreciate all the Shaykh says in *Futūḥ al-ghayb. Sirr al-asrār* is the gateway to that city of knowledge.

By translating this book into English, Shaykh Tosun Bayrak has done a great service to those who do not know Arabic or cannot find the text in its original language. If Allah wills, this work will illuminate many souls, and lead those who have already received illumination into the higher regions of knowledge.

May Allah shower blessings on the soul of Ḥaḍrat Abdul-Qādir al-Jīlānī, may Allah be pleased with him, and lead all of us into that deeper and higher realm of knowledge, so that we may all be raised to the status of those 'closest to Allah.'

Syed Ali Ashraf
Director General
The Islamic Academy
Cambridge

Translator's Introduction

THE venerable Muḥyiddīn Abū Muḥammad ʿAbdul-Qādir al-Jīlānī, may his soul be sanctified, is *al-ghawth al-aʿẓam*—the manifestation of Allah's attribute 'the All-Powerful', who hears the cry for help and saves the ones in need, and *al-quṭb al-aʿẓam*—the pole, the centre, the summit of spiritual evolution, the spiritual ruler of the world, the source of wisdom, container of all knowledge, the example of faith and Islam; a true inheritor of the perfection of the Prophet Muḥammad ﷺ; a perfect man; and the founder of the Qādiriyya, the mystical order that has spread far and wide and preserved the true meaning of Islamic Sufism throughout these centuries until our time.

He was born in 470 A.H. (1077–78 C.E.), in the region called al-Jīl in what is today Iran. This date is based on his statement to his son that he was eighteen when he went to Baghdad, in the year that the famous scholar al-Tamīmī died. This was 488 A.H. His mother, Ummul-Khayr Fāṭima bint al-Shaykh ʿAbdullāh Sūmī, was from the line of the Prophet Muḥammad ﷺ, through his grandson, the venerable Ḥusayn.

His mother relates,

> My son ʿAbdul-Qādir was born in the month of Ramaḍān. No matter how hard I tried, he refused to suckle in the daytime. Throughout his infancy he would never take food during the month of fasting.

One Ramaḍān during his infancy the start of the month fell on a cloudy day when people could not see the new moon. Not knowing if the month of fasting had actually begun or not, they came to Ummul-Khayr and asked if the child had taken food that day. As he had not, they surmised that the fast had begun.

The venerable ʿAbdul-Qādir relates,

> When I was a small child, every day I was visited by an angel in the shape of a beautiful young man. He would walk with me from our house to school and make the children in the class give me a place in the first row. He would stay with me the whole day and then bring me back home. I would learn in a single day more than the other students learned in a week. I did not know who he was. One day I asked him and he said, 'I am one of Allah's angels. He sent me to you and asked me to be with you as long as you study.'

Speaking again about his childhood, he relates,

> Each time I felt a desire to go and play with other children I would hear a voice saying, 'Come to Me instead, O blessed one, come to Me'. In terror I would go and seek the comfort of my mother's arms. Now, even in my most intense devotions and long seclusions, I cannot hear that voice as clearly.

When he was asked by someone what brought him to his high spiritual level, he said, 'The truthfulness which I promised to my mother.' He related the following story:

> One day, on the eve of ʿId al-Aḍḥā , I went to our fields to help till the ground. As I was walking behind the ox, it turned its head and looked at me and said, 'You were not created for this!' I was very afraid and ran home and climbed up on our flat roof. As I looked out I saw the pilgrims gathered on the plain of ʿArafāt, in Arabia, right in front of me.
>
> I went to my mother, who was then a widow, and asked her, 'Send me to the path of Truth, give me permission

to go to Baghdad to acquire knowledge, to be with the wise and those who are close to Allah.' My mother asked me what was the reason for this sudden request. I told her what had happened to me. She cried, but she brought out eighty pieces of gold, which was all that my father had left as inheritance. She put aside forty pieces for my brother. The other forty she sewed into the armpit of my coat. Then she permitted me to leave, but before she let me go she made me promise her that I would tell the truth and be truthful, whatever happened. She sent me off with these words: 'May Allah protect and guide you, my son. I separate myself from that which is dearest to me for Allah's sake. I know that l will not be able to see you until the day of Last Judgment.'

I joined a small caravan going to Baghdad. As we left behind the city of Hamadān, a band of highwaymen, sixty horsemen strong, attacked us. They took everything that everyone had. One of these came to me and asked, 'Young man, what possessions do you have?' I told him that I had forty pieces of gold. He said, 'Where?' I told him, 'Under my armpit'. He laughed and left me alone. Another bandit came and asked the same, and I told him the truth. He also left me alone. They must have repeated the incident to their leader, because he called me to the place where they were dividing the booty. He asked if I had any valuables. I told him that I had forty pieces of gold sewn in my coat under my arm. He took my coat, tore the armpit, and found the gold. Then he asked me in amazement, 'When your money was safe, what compelled you to insist on telling us that you had it and where it was hidden?' I answered, 'I must tell the truth under any circumstances, as I promised to my mother.' When the chief of the bandits heard this he wept and said, 'I reneged on my promise to the One Who created me. I stole and killed. What will happen to me?' And the others, seeing him, said, 'You have been our leader all these years in sinning. Now be also our leader in repenting!' All sixty of them held my

> hand and repented and changed their ways. Those sixty are the first who took my hand and found forgiveness for their sins.

When the venerable ʿAbdul-Qādir came to Baghdad, he was eighteen years old. As he reached the gates of the city, Khiḍr appeared and prevented him from entering. He told him that it was Allah's order that he not enter Baghdad for another seven years.

Khiḍr took him to a ruin in the desert and said, 'Stay here and do not leave this place'. He remained there three years. Every year Khiḍr would appear to him and tell him to stay where he was.

The saint tells about these years:

> During my stay in the deserts outside Baghdad, all that appears beautiful but is temporal and of this world came to seduce me. Allah protected me from their harm. The Devil, appearing in different forms and shapes, kept coming to me, tempting me, bothering me, and fighting me. Allah rendered me victorious over him. My ego visited me daily in my own form and shape, begging me to be its friend. When I would refuse, it would attack me. Allah rendered me victorious in my continuous fight against it. In time I was able to make it my prisoner and I kept it with me all those years, forcing it to stay in the ruins of the desert. A whole year I ate the grasses and roots I could find and did not drink any water. Another year I drank water but didn't eat a morsel of food. Another year I neither ate, nor drank, nor slept. All this time I lived in the ruins of the ancient kings of Persia in Karkh. I walked barefoot over the desert thorns and didn't feel a thing. Whenever I saw a cliff, I climbed it; I didn't give a minute's rest or comfort to my ego, to the low desires of my flesh.
>
> At the end of seven years I heard a voice at night: 'O ʿAbdul-Qādir, you are now permitted to enter Baghdad'.
>
> I came to Baghdad and spent a few days there. Soon I could not stand the sedition, mischief, and intrigue that dominated

the city. To save myself from the harm of this degenerate city and to save my faith, I left. All I took with me was my Qur'ān. As I came to the gate of the city, on my way to seclusion in the desert, I heard a voice. 'Where are you going?' it said, 'Return. You must serve the people.'

'What do I care about the people?' I protested. 'I have my faith to save!'

'Return, and never fear for your faith,' the voice continued, 'Nothing will ever harm you.' I could not see the one who spoke.

Then something happened to me. Cut off from the outside, I fell into an inner state of meditation. Until the next day I concentrated on a wish and prayed to Allah that He might part the veils for me so that I knew what should be done.

The next day, as I was wandering through a neighbourhood called Muẓaffariyya, a man whom I had never seen opened the door of his house and called to me, 'Come in, ʿAbdul-Qādir!' As I came to his door, he said, 'Tell me, what did you wish from Allah? What did you pray for yesterday?' I was frozen, with amazement. I could not find words to answer him. The man looked at my face and slammed the door with such violence that the dust was raised all around me and covered me from head to foot. I walked away, wondering what I had asked from Allah the day before. Then I remembered. I turned back to tell the man, but I could find neither the house nor him. I was very worried, as I realized he was a man close to Allah. In fact, later I was to learn that he was Ḥammād al-Dabbās, who became my shaykh.

On a cold and rainy night an invisible hand led Ḥaḍrat ʿAbdul-Qādir to the *tekke*, the mystical lodge, of Shaykh Hammād ibn Muslim al-Dabbās. The shaykh, knowing by divine inspiration of his coming, had the doors of the lodge shut and the lights put out. As ʿAbdul-Qādir sat at the sill of the locked door, sleep came upon him. He had a nocturnal emission and went and bathed himself at the river and took his ablution. He fell asleep again and the same thing happened—seven times during that night. Each time he bathed and took ablution in the ice-cold water. In the morning the gates were opened and he entered the Sufi lodge. Shaykh Hammād stood up to greet him. Weeping with joy, he embraced him and said, 'O my son ʿAbdul-Qādir, good fortune is ours today, but tomorrow it will be yours. Do not ever leave this path.' Shaykh Ḥammād became his first teacher in the sciences of mysticism. It was by holding his hand that he took his vows and entered the path of the Sufis.

He relates:

> I studied with many teachers in Baghdad, but whenever I couldn't understand something or came upon a secret that I wished to know, it was Shaykh al-Dabbās who would enlighten me. Sometimes I would leave him to seek knowledge from others—to learn theology, traditions, religious law, and other sciences. Each time I returned he would tell me, 'Where have you been? We have had so much wonderful food for our bodies, minds, and souls while you were gone and we haven't kept a thing for you!' At other times he would say, 'For Allah's sake, where do you go? Is there anyone around here who knows more than you do?' His dervishes would tease me continuously and say, 'You are a man of law and a man of letters, a man of knowledge, a scientist. What business do you have among us? Why don't you get out of here?' And the shaykh would chide them and say, 'Shame on you! I swear that there is none like him among you. None of you will rise above his toe! If you think I am harsh with him and you imitate me, I do it to bring him to perfection and to test him. I see him in the spiritual realm sturdy as a rock, as big as a mountain.'

Ḥaḍrat ʿAbdul-Qādir was the greatest example of the fact that in Islam, to seek knowledge is a sacred obligation—for all men and women, from the cradle to the grave. He sought out the greatest wise men of his time. He memorized the Holy Qur'ān and studied its interpretation from 'Alī Abūl-Wafā al-Qayl, Abūl-Khaṭṭāb Maḥfūẓ, and Abūl-Ḥasan Muḥammad al-Qāḍī. According to some sources, he studied with Qāḍī Abū Saʿīd al-Mubārak ibn ʿAlī al-Muḥarramī, the greatest man of knowledge of his time in Baghdad. Although Ḥaḍrat ʿAbdul-Qādir learned the sciences of the mystic path from Shaykh Hammād al-Dabbās and entered the Sufi path by his hand, he was given the dervish cloak, the symbol of the mantle of the Prophet ﷺ, by Qāḍī Abū Saʿīd. The spiritual lineage of Qāḍī Abū Saʿīd passes through Shaykh Abūl-Ḥasan ʿAlī ibn Muḥammad al-Qurashī, Abūl-Faraj al-Ṭarsūsī, al-Tamīmī, Shaykh Abu Bakr al-Shiblī, Abūl-Qāsim al-Junayd, Sari al-Saqaṭī, Maʿrūf al-Karkhī, Dawūd al-Ṭā'ī, Ḥabīb al-ʿAjamī, and Ḥasan al-Baṣrī, to Ḥaḍrat ʿAlī ibn Abī Ṭālib. Ḥaḍrat ʿAlī took the cloak of service from the hands of Muḥammad ﷺ, the Beloved of the Lord of the Universe, and he from the archangel Gabriel, and he from the Divine Truth.

Someone asked Shaykh ʿAbdul-Qādir what he received from Allah Most High. He answered, 'Good conduct and knowledge.' Qādī Abū Saʿīd al-Muḥarramī said, 'Indeed, ʿAbdul-Qādir al-Jīlānī took the dervishes' cloak from my hand, but I as well received my cloak of service from his hand.'

Abū Saʿīd al-Muḥarramī taught at a school of his own at Bab al-ʿAzj in Baghdad. Later he gave that school to Shaykh ʿAbdul-Qādir, who began to teach there.

Shaykh ʿAbdul-Qādir was over fifty years old by that time. His words were so effective and miraculous that they transformed the ones who heard them. His students and congregation increased in number very rapidly. Soon there was no place either in or around the school to accommodate his followers.

Shaykh ʿAbdul-Qādir tells about the beginning of his teaching:

> One morning I saw the Messenger of Allah. He asked me, 'Why do you not speak?'

I said, 'I am but a Persian, how can I speak with the beautiful Arabic of Baghdad?'

'Open your mouth,' He said. I did. He blew his breath seven times in my mouth and said, 'Go, address mankind and invite them to the path of your Lord with wise and beautiful words.'

I performed my noon prayer, and turned to see many people waiting for me to speak. When I saw them I became excited and tongue-tied. Then I saw the blessed Imam 'Alī. He came to me and asked me to open my mouth, then blew his own breath into it six times. I asked, 'Why did you not blow seven times like the Messenger of Allah?' He said, 'Because of my respect for him,' and disappeared.

From my open mouth came the words, 'The mind is a diver, diving deep into the sea of the heart to find the pearls of wisdom. When he brings them to the shore of his being, they spill out as words from his lips, and with these he buys priceless devotions in Allah's markets of worship...' Then I said, 'In a night such as one of mine, if one of you should kill his low desires, that death would taste so sweet that he would not be able to taste anything else in this world!'

From then on, whether I was awake or asleep I kept my duty in teaching. There was such an immense amount of knowledge about faith and religion in me. If I did not talk and pour it out, I felt that it would drown me. When I started teaching I had only two or three students. When they heard me, their numbers increased to seventy thousand.

Neither his school nor its vicinity could contain his followers. More space had to be found. Rich and poor helped in adding buildings, the rich aiding financially and the poor helping with their labour. The women of Baghdad also worked. A young woman who was working as a labourer without pay brought her husband, who was unwilling to work for nothing, and presented him to the shaykh. 'This is my husband,' she said. 'I took twenty pieces of gold from him as dowry. I will give half of it back to him free, and for the other half I wish him to work here.' She gave Ḥaḍrat ʿAbdul-Qādir the gold, and the man started working. He did not stop when the money ran out. Nonetheless the shaykh kept paying him, because he knew that he was needy.

Ḥaḍrat ʿAbdul-Qādir al-Jīlānī was the authority, the imam, in religious matters, theology and law, and the leader of the Shāfiʿī and Ḥanbalī branches of Islam. He was a man of great wisdom and knowledge. All men profited from him. His prayers were immediately accepted, both when he prayed for good and when he prayed for punishment. He performed many miracles. He was a perfect man, of continuous consciousness and remembrance of Allah, meditating, thinking, taking and giving lessons.

He had a soft heart, a gentle nature and a smiling face. He was sensitive and possessed the best of manners. He was aristocratic in character, generous and giving both of material things and of advice and knowledge. He loved people, but especially those who were believers and who served and worshipped the One in Whom they believed.

He was handsome and well-dressed. He did not speak excessively, but when he did speak, though he spoke fast, every single word and syllable was clear. He spoke beautifully and he spoke the truth. He spoke the truth without fear, for he did not care whether he was praised or criticized and condemned.

When the Caliph al-Muqtafī appointed Yaḥyā ibn Saʿīd as Qāḍī, or Chief Justice, Ḥaḍrat ʿAbdul-Qādir accused him in public, saying, 'You have appointed the worst tyrant as judge over the believers. Let us see how you will answer for yourself tomorrow when you will be presented to the Great Judge, the Lord of the Universe!' Hearing this, the caliph started to shake and shed tears. The judge was immediately dismissed.

The population of the city of Baghdad was degenerate in its morals and behaviour. Through his influence, most of the city's people repented, and followed the good morals and prescriptions of Islam. He came to be loved and respected by everyone, and his influence spread everywhere. As the righteous loved him, so tyrants and wrongdoers feared him. Many people, including kings, viziers, and wise men, came to him to ask questions and seek solutions. Many Jews and Christians accepted Islam through him.

There was a very wise and influential priest in Baghdad who had many followers. This man had vast knowledge not only of the Judaic and Christian traditions but also of Islam; He knew Islam and the Holy Qur'ān and had great love and appreciation for the Prophet Muḥammad ﷺ. The caliph respected the priest and hoped that he and his followers would become Muslims one day. Indeed, he was ready to accept the religion, except for one thing. The thing that prevented him, which he could neither accept nor understand, was the physical ascension of the Prophet Muḥammad ﷺ to the heavens during his lifetime.

The Ascension took place when one night, the Prophet ﷺ was brought body and soul from Medina to Jerusalem and from there to the seven heavens, where he saw many things. He visited Paradise and Hell, and went beyond these to meet his Lord, Who spoke ninety thousand words with him. He returned before his bed had cooled, and before a leaf which he had touched in passing had stopped trembling.

The mind of the priest could not accept the ascension of the Prophet and his coming back to tell about it. Indeed, when the Prophet ﷺ himself declared it the day after it happened, many Muslims did not believe and left their religion. This then is a test of true faith, for the mind cannot conceive of such a thing.

The caliph introduced all the wise men and teachers of his time to the priest in order to eliminate his doubts, but none of them succeeded. Then one evening he sent word to Ḥaḍrat ʿAbdul-Qādir, asking him if he could convince the priest of the truth of the Ascension.

When Ḥaḍrat ʿAbdul-Qādir came to the palace he found the priest and the caliph playing chess. As the priest lifted a chess piece to move it, his eyes met those of the shaykh. He blinked his eyes... and as he opened them again he found himself drowning in a rapidly running river! He was shouting for help when a young shepherd jumped into the water to save him. As the shepherd held onto him, he realized that he was naked and had been transformed into a young girl!

The shepherd pulled her out of the water and asked her whose daughter she was and where she lived. When the priest mentioned Baghdad, the shepherd said that they were then at a distance of a few months journey from that city. The shepherd honoured her and kept her and protected her, but eventually as she had nowhere to go, he married her. They had three children, who grew up.

One day as she was washing laundry in the same river where she had appeared many years before, she slipped and fell in. As she opened her eyes... he found himself sitting across from the caliph, holding the chess piece and still looking up into the eyes of Ḥaḍrat ʿAbdul-Qādir, who said to him, 'Now, venerable priest, do you still disbelieve?'

The priest, unsure of what had happened to him and thinking that it was a dream, responded with the words, 'What do you mean?'

'Perhaps you would like to see your family?' the saint inquired. As he opened the door, there stood the shepherd and the three children.

Seeing this, the priest believed. He and his congregation number among the five thousand Christians who became Muslim by the hands of Ḥaḍrat ʿAbdul-Qādir.

In his teaching and his service to mankind he applied qualities which he inherited from the highest. He said,

> A spiritual teacher is not a true teacher unless he possesses twelve qualities. Two of these qualities are from the attributes of Allah Most High. They are to hide the faults of man and the rest of creation, not only from others, but even from themselves and to have compassion and forgiveness for even the worst of sins. Two qualities are inherited from the Prophet Muḥammad ﷺ— love and gentleness. From Ḥaḍrat Abū Bakr, the first of the four Caliphs, a true teacher inherits truthfulness,

honesty and sincerity, as well as devotion and generosity. From Ḥaḍrat 'Umar, justice, and imposing the right and preventing the wrong. From Ḥaḍrat 'Uthmān, humility, and staying awake and praying while the rest of mankind are asleep. From Ḥaḍrat 'Alī, knowledge and courage.

He was as devoted as a father to all his tens of thousands of followers. He knew them by name, and cared for their worldly affairs as well as their spiritual state. He helped them and saved them from disasters, even if they were at the other end of the world. He was a child with the children, and treated them with the utmost tenderness and compassion. With those much older than he, he became as if older than they, and treated them with respect.

He kept the company of the poor and the weak; he did not seek the company of the famous and powerful. With such people he behaved as if he were the king's own King.

One of the sons of his servant related that his father, Muḥammad Ibn al-Khiḍr, served Shaykh ʿAbdul-Qādir for thirteen years. He never saw a fly sit on him, nor did he ever see him blow his nose. Although the shaykh treated the weak and the poor with great respect, his servant never saw him get up when sultans came to visit him, neither did he visit them, nor did he eat their food except once. When a king came to visit him he would leave the reception room and would come back after the king and his party were settled, so that they would greet him by standing up. When he wrote a letter to the caliph he would say that ʿAbdul-Qādir orders him to do this or that, and that it was an obligation for the caliph to obey him, since he was their leader. When the caliph received such a letter he would kiss it before he read it and say, 'The shaykh is right, indeed he is telling the truth!'

One of the great jurists of the time, Abū-Ḥasan, relates:

I heard the caliph al-Muqtafī tell his minister Ibn Hubayra, 'Shaykh ʿAbdul-Qādir is ridiculing me, making it clear to those around him that he means me. It was reported to me that he pointed at a date-palm in his orchard and said, "You'd better behave. Don't go too far or I will behead you!" Go to him and talk to him alone and say, "You should not ridicule and threaten the caliph. You must know that the station of the caliph is sacred and has to be respected."

The vizier Ibn Hubayra went to the shaykh and found him in the company of a vast crowd. In his talk, at one point he suddenly declared, "Indeed, I would behead him, too!" The vizier felt that the shaykh meant him, and terrified, he fled and told what had happened to the caliph. The caliph was brought to tears and said, "Truly, the shaykh is great." He went to see him himself. The shaykh gave him much advice and the caliph cried and cried.'

Although he was most compassionate and had the best character and manners—gentle and loving, keeping his promises—he was just, and stern in his justice. He never showed anger because of anything done to him, but if any wrongful act were committed against the faith and the religion, in his anger he would become awesome and his punishment would be swift and hard.

A shaykh of the time, Abū-Najīb al-Suhrawardī, relates:

In the year 523 Hijri I was with Shaykh Ḥammād, the teacher of Shaykh ʿAbdul-Qādir, who was also present. Shaykh ʿAbdul-Qādir made a grand statement. At that Shaykh Ḥammād told him, 'O ʿAbdul-Qādir, you talk too loftily! I fear for you the disapproval of Allah.'

ʿAbdul-Qādir put his hand on the chest of Shaykh Ḥammād. 'Look at my palm with the eye of your heart,' he said, 'and tell me what is written on it' When Shaykh Ḥammād could not say, ʿAbdul-Qādir lifted his hand from the shaykh's chest and showed the palm to him. On it was a luminous writing saying, 'He has received seventy promises from Allah that he will never be disappointed'.

When Shaykh Ḥammād saw this, he said, 'There could never be an objection to a man blessed with such a divine promise. No one could ever object to him. Allah blesses whom ever He wills among His servants.'

Shaykh ʿAbdul-Qādir used to say:

None of my followers will die before they repent. They will all die as faithful servants of Allah. Each of my good followers will save seven of his sinful brothers from hellfire. If, in the far west, the private parts of one of my followers were to be inadvertently exposed, we, although we were in the far east, would cover them before anyone could notice.

I have been given a book, a book as long as any eye could see, which contains all the names of the ones who will follow me until the end of time. With Allah's blessing we will save all of them. Blessed are those who see me. I yearn for the ones who will not see me.

All those who attached themselves to him were always at peace and joyful. Someone asked him, 'We know the state of your good followers and what awaits them in the Hereafter. But what about the bad ones?' He answered, 'The good ones are devoted to me and I am devoted to saving the bad ones.'

A young girl who was a follower of the shaykh lived in Ceylon. One day she was attacked in a lonely place by a man intending to dishonour her. Helpless, she shouted, 'Save me, O my shaykh ʿAbdul-Qādir!' At that moment the shaykh was taking his ablution in Baghdad. People saw him stop, angrily grab his wooden shoe, and throw it in the air. They did not see the shoe fall down. That shoe fell on the head of the villain who was attacking the girl in Ceylon, and killed him. It is said that the shoe is still there, kept as a relic.

Sahl ibn 'Abdullah al-Tustarī relates that one day Shaykh ʿAbdul-Qādir's followers in Baghdad lost him. They looked everywhere for him. Someone told them he had been seen going toward the Tigris River, and his followers ran there after him. When they arrived at the river, he was in the midst of it, walking over the water towards them. All the fish were putting their heads out of the water and giving him greeting.

It was the time of the noon prayer. They saw above them a vast carpet spread over their heads, covering the whole sky. It was a green carpet, and on it in gold and silver were embroidered the words:

> *Indeed for the friends of Allah there is neither fear nor sorrow.* (Sūra Yūnus, 62) *O family of the Prophet, Allah's peace and blessings be upon you. Indeed He alone is praiseworthy and most glorious* (Sūra Hūd, 73)

The carpet floated like the flying carpet of the prophet Solomon, and descended to the ground. The people, inspired, quiet and peaceful, walked towards it. The shaykh, clad in beautiful clothes, stepped upon the carpet and led them in prayer upon it. When he raised his hands and said, 'Allah is great,' the whole sky echoed the same words. As he prayed, the angels of the seven heavens in chorus repeated his prayers. When he said, 'All praise is due to Allah,' a green light emanated from his mouth, covering the sky. At the end of the prayer he opened his hands and said, 'O Lord, for the sake of my ancestor your beloved Muḥammad, peace be upon him, and for the sake of those among your creation who fear and love you, do not take any of my followers to you until they are forgiven of their sins and until their faith is complete.' One and all heard the hum of the angels saying, 'Amīn.' Following the angels, they too said 'Amīn.' Then they all heard a voice from inside of them saying, 'Rejoice! I have accepted your prayers.'

The Prophet Muḥammad ﷺ says, 'The perfect shaykh is like a prophet to his people'. Indeed Ḥaḍrat ʿAbdul-Qādir was one of those perfect shaykhs who opened to people the gates of felicity in this world and the gates of Paradise in the next.

It was only after Ḥaḍrat ʿAbdul-Qādir had mastered his ego and become a perfect man, and only by the inspired command of the Holy Prophet ﷺ, that he became a teacher and established contact with the people. It was also at this time that, following the example of his ancestor the Prophet Muḥammad ﷺ, he married four wives, each a model of virtue and devoted to him. He was fifty-one years old, He had forty-nine children: twenty-seven sons and twenty-two daughters.

One day his wives came to him and said, 'O possessor of the best of characters, your little son has died, and we haven't seen a single tear in your eyes, nor have you shown any sign of sadness or concern. Don't you have any compassion for someone who is a part of you? We are bent over double in sorrow, yet you go about your business as if nothing has happened. You are our master, our guide, our hope for this world and the Hereafter, but if your heart is hard and there is no compassion there, how can we, who hope to hold onto you on the day of Last Judgment, have faith that you will save us?'

The shaykh said, 'O my dear friends, do not think that my heart is hard. I pity the unfaithful for his unfaithfulness, I pity the dog who bites me and pray to Allah that it stop biting people, not that I mind being bitten, but because others will throw stones at it. Don't you know that I have inherited compassion from the one whom Allah sent as mercy upon the universe?'

The women said, 'Indeed, if you have feeling even for the dog which bites you, how is it that you do not show any feeling for your own son who has been smitten with the sword of death?'

The shaykh said, 'O my sad companions, you cry because you feel separated from your son whom you love. I am always with the one I love. You saw your son in the dream which this world is, and you have lost him in another dream. Allah says, "This world is but a dream." It is a dream for the ones who are asleep. I am awake. I saw my son when he was within the circle of time. Now he has walked out of that circle. I still see him and he is with me. He is playing around me just as he did before. For when you see that which is real with the eye of the heart, whether dead or alive, the truth does not disappear.'

One day the shaykh and some of his followers were travelling on foot in the desert. It was the month of Ramaḍān and the desert was hot. He related:

> I was exceedingly tired and thirsty. My followers were walking ahead of me. All of a sudden a cloud appeared overhead, like an umbrella protecting us from the hot sun. In front of us appeared a gushing spring and a date-palm laden with ripe fruit. Finally there came a round light, brighter than the sun and standing apart from it. A voice came from its direction. It said, 'O people of Abdul-Qādir, I am your Lord! Eat and drink, for I have made lawful for you what I have made unlawful for others!' My people, who were ahead of me, rushed to the spring to drink, and to the date-palm to eat from it. I shouted at them to stop, and lifting my head towards the direction of the voice I shouted, 'I take refuge in Allah from the accursed Devil!'
>
> The cloud, the light, the spring and the date-palm all disappeared. The Devil stood in front of us in all his ugliness. He asked, 'How did you know that it was me?' I told the Accursed One who has been thrown out of Allah's mercy that the address of Allah is not a sound heard with the ears, nor does it come from outside. Furthermore, I knew that Allah's laws are constant and are meant for all. He neither changes them, nor renders that which is unlawful lawful to the ones He favours.
>
> Upon hearing this, the Devil tried his last temptation of arousing pride. 'O ʿAbdul-Qādir,' he said, 'I have fooled seventy prophets with this trick. Your knowledge is vast, your wisdom is greater than that of the prophets!' Then pointing to my followers he went on, 'Is this handful of fools your only following? The whole world should follow you, for you are as good as a prophet.'
>
> I said, 'I take refuge from you in my Lord Who is All-hearing and All-knowing. For it is not my knowledge, nor my wisdom, which saved me from you, but the mercy of my Lord.'

He saw everything as from Allah, did everything for Allah's sake, and attributed nothing to any created being, including himself.

What he said, he did. Compliment or criticism, benefit or loss, were the same to him. His knowledge was all-encompassing and his wisdom supreme. He considered the ones who know and do not apply their knowledge as no better than donkeys carrying heavy books.

One of the great shaykhs of the time, Shaykh Muẓaffar Manṣūr ibn al-Mubārak al-Wāsiṭī, relates:

> I came to visit Shaykh ʿAbdul-Qādir with some of my students. I was carrying a book on philosophy in my hand. He greeted us and looked at us, then said to me, 'What a bad and dirty friend you are holding in your hand! Go and wash it!' I was awed by the shaykh's angry words. He could not have known the contents of the book, which I loved and which I had almost memorized.
>
> I debated with myself whether to get up and hide the book somewhere and pick it up on my departure. As I was about to go and do this, he gave me a strange look and I couldn't lift myself from my seat. He ordered me to give the book to him. As I was doing so I opened it for a last look. I saw only empty white pages! All that was written had disappeared.
>
> I gave the book to him. He took it, browsed through it, and gave it back to me, saying, 'Here it is, "The Wisdom of the Qur'ān" by Ibn Dāris.' I took it and opened it, and indeed the book of philosophy had been transformed into *Faḍā'il al-Qur'ān* by Ibn Dāris, written in the most beautiful calligraphy. Then he said to me, 'Do you wish your heart to repent when you voice your repentance?' I answered, 'Indeed I do'. He said, 'Then stand up'. As I rose to stand, I felt all of my knowledge of philosophy descend from my mind and sink to the ground. Not a word of it remained in my memory.

Another time a great number of people gathered around Shaykh ʿAbdul-Qādir, hoping that he would speak. He sat for a very long time without saying a word; the congregation also sat and waited silently. After a while a strange ecstasy overcame them, as if they had been emptied of all thought and imagination. Then all of them together thought the same thing: 'What is the shaykh thinking about?'

As soon as this question was raised in their minds, Ḥaḍrat ʿAbdul-Qādir spoke. 'Just now a man was transported from Mecca to Baghdad in an instant, repented in my presence, and flew back,' he said.

The congregation thought as one: 'Why should a man who could fly in an instant from Mecca to Baghdad need to repent?'

He said, 'To fly in the air is one thing, but to feel love is something else. I taught him how to love.'

ʿAbdullāh Zayal relates:

> In the year 560 I was at the school of Ḥaḍrat ʿAbdul-Qādir. One day I saw him leaving his house with his staff in his hand. I said to myself, 'I wish he would show me a miracle with that staff!' He looked at me and smiled and stuck the staff into the sand. Instantly it turned into a beam of intense light rising out of sight into the sky, illuminating everything for an hour. Then he held that beam of light. It turned back into an ordinary staff. He looked at me and said, 'O Zayal, is that all that you wanted?'

At his hands more than five thousand Jews and Christians became Muslims. More than a hundred thousand ruffians, outlaws, murderers, thieves, and bandits repented and became devout Muslims and gentle dervishes. He explains how he reached that blessed state.

> For twenty-five years I wandered in the deserts of Iraq. I slept in ruins. In a place at Shustar, a ruined castle in the middle of the desert twelve days' journey from Baghdad, I stayed in seclusion for eleven years. I promised my Lord that I would neither eat nor drink until I reached spiritual perfection. On the fortieth day a man came with a loaf of bread and some

food and placed them in front of me and disappeared. My flesh screamed, 'I am hungry, I am hungry!' My ego whispered, 'Your promise is fulfilled. Why don't you eat?' But I did not break my vow to Allah.

By chance the scholar Abū Sa'īd al-Muḥarramī happened to be passing by. He heard the screams of hunger of my flesh, though I was deaf to them. He came and saw my emaciated state and said to me, 'What is this I see and hear, Oᶜ Abdul-Qādir?'

'Don't mind it, my friend,' I said. 'It is only the voice of the disobedient, unruly ego, while, I tell you, the soul is bowed in front of its Lord and is hopeful and peaceful and joyful.'

'Please come to my school at Bāb al-'Azj,' he asked. I did not answer, but inwardly I said, 'I will not leave this place without divine order.' Not long after Khiḍr came to me and told me, 'Go and join Abu Sa'īd'.

When I received the order, I went to Baghdad, to the school of Abu Sa'īd, and found him waiting for me at the gate. 'I begged you to come!' he said. Then he invested me with the cloak of the dervish. From that time on I never left him.

Forty years I never slept at night. I made my morning prayer with the ablution I had taken to make my night prayer. I read the Qur'ān every night so that sleep should not overtake me. I stood on one foot and leaned against the wall with one hand. I did not change this position until I had read the whole Qur'ān.

When I could not fight sleep myself, I would hear a voice that shook every cell in my body. It would say, 'O ᶜAbdul-Qādir, I did not create you to sleep! You were nothing. I gave you life. So while you are alive you will not be unaware of Us.'

One day someone asked him, 'O ᶜAbdul-Qādir, we pray, fast and deny the low desires of our flesh just like you. How is it that we do not receive high mystical states and the ability to perform miracles, as you do?'

He answered, 'I see that not only do you try to compete with me in actions—thinking that you do what I do while you merely do what you see me do—but you reproach Allah for not giving you the same rewards! Allah is my witness that I have never eaten or drunk unless I heard my Creator say, "Eat and drink—you owe it to Me for the body I have given you." Neither have I done a single thing without the order of my Lord.'

Shaykh 'Alī ibn Musāfir relates:

> I was among thousands of people gathered to hear him in the open air. As he spoke, a heavy rain started pouring down and some people started to leave. The sky was dark with clouds promising more rain. Ḥaḍrat ʿAbdul-Qādir lifted his head and his hands in prayer and said, 'O Lord, I try to gather people for You. Are You trying to chase them away from me?' As soon as he said this, it stopped raining on us. Not a drop fell on us until he finished speaking, though it was pouring outside the place we were gathered.

Yaḥyā ibn Jina al-Adīb recalled:

> Shaykh ʿAbdul-Qādir used to interject poetry into his talks. One day he was talking about the soul and he recited the poem,
>
> My soul, before it came to be in the realm of
>   nothingness, loved You.
> If I withdrew from the realm of love, now,
> Would my feet carry me away?
>
> Inwardly I said to myself, 'Let's see how many poems he will recite today.' I had a piece of thread with me and I put a knot in it under my cloak each time he recited a verse. I was sitting far away from him. He could not possibly have seen me. He looked at me and said, 'I try to unravel, and you seem to tie knots!'

His devout servant Abūl-Riḍā relates:

One day, while preaching, the shaykh stopped in the middle of a sentence and declared, 'I will not continue unless you give me a hundred pieces of gold right now!' Quickly people gathered a hundred dinars and placed them in my hands. Everyone was shocked, not knowing what to do, looking at him in amazement. I brought him the money. He gave the hundred dinars back to me and said, 'O Abūl-Riḍā, go to the cemetery of Shūnīziyyah. You will find there an old man playing a lute to the graves. Give this gold to him and bring him to me.'

I went, and indeed, there was an old man playing his lute and singing to the tombs. I offered him salutations and gave him the bag of gold. He was awestruck, gave a long scream, and fainted.

When he revived I brought him to Shaykh ʿAbdul-Qādir, who asked him to come up to the pulpit. The man climbed the steps with the lute on his shoulders. 'Friend, tell them your story,' the shaykh said.

The lute-player told us that he had been a popular singer of fame in his youth. Yet when he grew old no one sought him or wished to hear him anymore. Sad and abandoned by everybody, that very day he had vowed he would never sing to anyone but the dead. He had come to the cemetery and as he sat there singing and playing his lute the grave nearest him split open! The dead man raised his head and said, 'All your life you have sung for the dead. Sing for once for the Ever-living, for Allah. He certainly will give you more than you have ever received—more than you ever hoped to receive!' When he saw and heard that, he fainted in fear and awe. Then, coming to himself, he began to sing:

> O My Lord, on the day I meet You I will have nothing to bring but begging on my lips and hope for mercy in my heart.

All will be gathered with hope in Your presence,
woe to me if I am left empty-handed!
If only the good come begging to Your gate, to
whom should sinners go, seeking?
O Lord, when I come to You in shame on the Day
of Reckoning, will You not save me from the
Fire?

Abūl-Riḍā further relates:

In the middle of the verse I came to him with the hundred dinars from my master as a reward for his entreaties to his Lord, and in amazement he fainted.

The lute-player, tears pouring from his eyes, repented. He threw down his lute and broke it. The shaykh said, 'If this is Allah's reward for the sincerity of someone who took this life as a game, what shall be the reward of the servant of Allah who is true and sincere all of his life? Keep sincerity in your heart, for without it you will not advance towards your Lord even an inch.'

ʿAbdul-Ṣamad ibn Humām was one of the wealthiest men in Baghdad. A worldly, proud, and arrogant man, he believed he owned the world and the people who worked for him. He supposed he could control them, doing with them whatever he pleased. A materialist in every sense of the word, he disliked the shaykh profoundly and denied his miracles. He relates:

As you know, I never liked the shaykh. Although I am a man of means and have all that I wish, I was never content, happy or at peace.

One Friday, as I was passing by his school, I heard the call to prayer. I said to myself, 'Let's take a closer look at this man who impresses others with his so-called miracles. I'll go and make my Friday prayer in his mosque.'

The mosque was packed solid. I pushed myself forward in the crowd and found a place right at the foot of the pulpit. The shaykh started delivering his sermon and the things he said angered me.

All of a sudden I had a terrible urgent need to relieve myself. There was no way out of the mosque. I was filled with horror at the terrible shame, as I was about to defecate right there and then. My anger toward the shaykh increased.

At that moment he calmly descended the steps of the pulpit and stood above me. While continuing to talk, he covered me with the skirt of his cloak. All of a sudden I found myself in a beautiful green valley where a pure brook flowed. There was no one around. I relieved myself and cleansed myself and took ablution in the brook. As I decided to make my prayer, I found myself again under the shaykh's cloak. He lifted it from me and returned up the steps of the pulpit.

I was awestruck. Not only was my belly comfortable but so was my heart. All the discontent, anger and negative feeling had been wiped out of it.

After the prayer I left the mosque and walked home. On the way, I realized that I had lost the key of my safe. I went back to the mosque and looked for it, but I couldn't find it anywhere. I had a hard time getting the locksmith to open my safe.

The next day I had to go on a business trip. Three days out of Baghdad we passed by a very beautiful valley. It was as if a force pulled us to the side of a beautiful brook. I realized immediately that this was the place I had been and the brook where I had washed myself. I washed myself again at the same place. There I found the lost key to my safe! When I returned to Baghdad I became a follower of the shaykh.

A woman of Baghdad, very impressed with the fame and wealth of the shaykh, decided to leave her son in the care of Ḥaḍrat ʿAbdul-Qādir. She brought the child to him and said, 'Take this child as your own—I renounce all right to him—and raise him to become like you' The shaykh accepted the child and started to teach him piety, asceticism and denial of the ego's low desires.

After some time the mother came to see her son and found him thin and pale and eating a crust of bread. She was angry at the shaykh and asked to see him. When she came upon him she found him well-dressed, seated in a pleasant room and eating a chicken. 'While you eat your chicken,' she reproached him, 'my poor son, whom I left in your care, has nothing but a piece of dry bread!'

The shaykh placed his hand over the bones of the chicken. 'In the name of Allah Who revives bones from dust, rise!' He lifted his hand and the chicken was alive. It ran about the table saying, 'There is no god but Allah and Muḥammad is His Messenger and Shaykh ʿAbdul-Qādir is the friend of Allah and His Messenger!'

The shaykh turned to the woman and said, 'When your son can do this, he can also eat whatever he wishes.'

One night, later in his life, fifty of the elite of Baghdad were gathered in his house. The company included all the great shaykhs of the time, among them Ḥāfiẓ Abūl-ʿIzz ʿAbdul-Mughīth ibn Ḥarb. He recalls:

> That night the shaykh was in a state of inspiration. Pearls of wisdom poured from his mouth. All of us were in a perfect state of peace and bliss, of a kind we had never experienced before. A moment came when the shaykh pointed to his foot and declared, 'This foot is over the necks of all the saints'. No sooner had he said this than one of his students, Shaykh ʿAlī ibn al-Ḥīlī, threw himself at his master's feet. He took the shaykh's foot and placed it upon his neck. Then all the rest of us did the same.

Another of those present, Shaykh Abū Saʿīd al-Kaylāwī, said:

> When he said, 'This foot is over the necks of all the saints,' I felt Allah's truth manifest in my heart. I saw all the saints of the world standing in his presence, filling my whole vision. The ones who were of this world were present bodily; those who

had passed away were present spiritually. The sky was filled with angels and other beings invisible to the eye. A group of angels descended and bestowed upon the saint the cloak of the Messenger of Allah ﷺ. As we all prostrated ourselves and stretched our necks we heard a soundless voice say 'O sultan of the time, guide of the religion, of the place, O executor of the word of Allah the Compassionate, inheritor of the Holy Book, deputy of Allah's Messenger, O he to whose orders the earth and the heavens are given, whose prayer is accepted, when he asks for rain the rain comes and milk comes from dry breasts, O beloved and respected of the whole creation. . . '

After Shaykh ʿAbdul-Qādir pronounced those words, not only those in his presence, but all the men of religion felt an increase in their knowledge and their wisdom, in the divine light in their hearts, and in their spiritual levels.

As this event became known all over the Muslim world, all the shaykhs and teachers put their heads on the floor in great humbleness and accepted his leadership. Sinners among the people came into his presence, repented, and became pure. Bandits, thieves, outlaws came to him and became his followers. He became the centre, the pole.

Three hundred and thirteen saints of the time, among them seventeen in the holy city of Mecca, sixty in Iraq, forty in Iran, twenty in Egypt, thirty in Damascus, eleven in Abyssinia, seven from Ceylon, twenty-seven in the West, forty-seven in the inaccessible lands beyond Mount Qāf, seven in the lands of Gog and Magog, and twenty-four in the islands of the oceans, all heard it and put their heads to the ground in obedience—with the exception of one Persian.

This Persian was a very devout shaykh. He prayed more than anyone and fasted continually. He made numerous pilgrimages to the Kaʿbah. He was very ambitious to obtain Allah's pleasure. For fifty years he remained in seclusion from the world with his four hundred disciples, whom he made work day and night to perfect themselves. He had great knowledge, and he could work miracles. When word of Ḥaḍrat ʿAbdul-Qādir's declaration reached him, he was at the Pilgrimage with his disciples, in the holy city of Mecca. Either he underestimated the greatness of Ḥaḍrat ʿAbdul-Qādir or he overestimated his own. He refused to lower his neck in obedience to ʿAbdul-Qādir's call. That night he dreamed that he went from Mecca to Byzantium and there he worshipped an idol. Depressed by this oppressive dream he gathered his disciples and said that he must go at once to Byzantium, where he hoped to discover the meaning of this dream. His loyal disciples followed him to Byzantium. As they entered the city the shaykh caught sight of a beautiful girl standing on a balcony. Her hair was black as night, her eyes were twin moons with arched brows like tender sickles over them, her look a lure for lovers, Her moist lips, the colour of rubies, rendered who looked upon them thirsty. Her mouth was so small that even words could not pass, her slender waist was clasped by the idolater's belt. As soon as the shaykh saw her his heart caught fire, his eyes became fixed on her, his will slipped from his hands. As his heart was filled with love for her, religion and faith left it. For all her beauty, that woman was a harlot, a temptation of the Devil. The shaykh stood at the door of this pagan harlot, his mouth open, his eyes fixed on the balcony, hoping to see her. Inwardly he was in torment. He thought that all these years he had fasted, had tormented his flesh, but never had he suffered like this. He sought his knowledge, his reason, to make sense out of this situation, but all reason and knowledge had left him. His companions came to him in terror and distress and begged him to come away, to repent, to pray. The shaykh replied that if he had to repent now, he would repent for the absurdity of giving up the world and its pleasures for the sake of his faith, and as for praying and begging, he would rather beg from this girl than from God. When he was reminded of Allah's punishment and Hell, he said that this separation from his beloved and the fire of love in his heart could feed seven Hells. His disciples pleaded with him for a long time, but seeing that their efforts produced no effect on the shaykh, they left him.

The shaykh stayed a whole month at the door of the pagan harlot. The dust was his bed and the doorstep his pillow. He slept on the street with the street dogs.

Finally the beautiful pagan came to her door to meet him and said to him, 'O old man who calls himself a shaykh and a Muslim, you are so drunk with the wine of giving partners to God that you show yourself in such a state in this pagan street!' The shaykh said, 'I will give up not only my religion but my life for one touch of your lips.' The harlot said, 'Shame on you, you old slave of your passions. How dare you suggest kissing me when you are ready to wrap yourself in your shroud and go to your tomb. Go away! I cannot love you.'

No matter how she insulted him, the shaykh stood at her door. Then she came down again and told him, 'If you love me as you say you do, then you must leave Islam, burn the Qur'ān, bow your head and prostrate yourself before the idols and drink wine.' He said, 'I cannot yet truly abandon Islam nor can I burn the Qur'ān, but I am willing to drink wine to your beauty.' She said, 'Then come and drink wine with me. You will soon agree to do all the other things which I ask of you.' As he sipped the wine from her hands, his heart and his mind blazed with fire. He tried to recall the Qur'ān which he had memorized, the books he had read and written on Islam, but he had forgotten them all. Drunk, he tried to touch her. She said, 'Not until you become a pagan like me and burn your Qur'ān.' He threw the Qur'ān and his dervish cloak into the fire, left his faith, and bowed to the pagan gods, and tried again to touch her. She said, 'You old dweller, slave of passion, who possesses neither worldly goods nor fame, how can a woman like me be caressed by such a beggar? I need silver and gold and silk. Since you have none, take your ugly self away!'

More time passed. The poor old man, wasted, stood at her gate. Finally, one day she gave herself to him. Then she said, 'Now for my price, O filthy old man, go and look after my herd of pigs for a year.' Without protest the one-time shaykh of the Kaʿbah became a swineherd.

The sad news of the shaykh who did not bow his head to Ḥaḍrat ʿAbdul-Qādir spread, and his disciples who had abandoned him reached Baghdad. They asked to see the shaykh. When they told him what had happened and that their shaykh had forsaken his religion, become a pagan and a swineherd, Ḥaḍrat ʿAbdul-Qādir said, 'If one does not submit and become a lamb to a shepherd, then one becomes a shepherd to a herd of pigs. For each man has his herd of a thousand pigs, a thousand idols in his heart, unless he drives them away by submission and repentance.' Then he reproached them for having left their shaykh and told them that they should even have become pagans for his sake! He added that a real friend is a friend upon whom you can rely in misfortune; in good fortune, everyone feigns to be your friend. Then the shaykh prayed for the misguided shaykh and told them to go back to Byzantium and tell him that ʿAbdul-Qādir bids him come back.

The disciples at once set out for Byzantium. They prayed for their shaykh all the way. They fasted and asked Allah to give their rewards to their shaykh. They sent numerous blessings to the Prophet Muḥammad ﷺ and asked for his intercession. The arrow of prayer reached its mark. When they came upon the shaykh they found him radiant among the many pigs, and when they told him of the call of Ḥaḍrat ʿAbdul-Qādir he tore away the girdle of the pagan, shed torrents of tears of remorse, lifted his hands to heaven in thankfulness, and all that he had forsaken—the Qur'ān, the divine secrets—came back to him and he was delivered from his misery and folly. Then he bathed himself and performed his ablutions and put on his dervish cloak and set out for Baghdad.

While all this was happening the pagan girl saw in a dream a light descending upon her and heard these words: 'Follow your shaykh, embrace his faith, be the dust beneath his feet. You who have been soiled are as pure as he is now. You led him in your way. Enter now into his.' When she awoke she was transformed. She rushed to catch up with the shaykh and his disciples. She ran, without eating or drinking, over mountains and plains. Finally, in the middle of the desert, she fell to the ground. She prayed, 'O You Who have created me, forgive me, do not strike me down. If I revolted against Your faith and Your ways, I did it in ignorance, as my shaykh did in arrogance. You forgave him, so forgive me. I submit and accept the true faith.'

Allah made the shaykh, who was not far away, hear her words and he and his disciples went back to where the girl lay. She said, 'I am consumed with shame because of you. Instruct me in Islam so that I may meet my Lord on the way.' As the shaykh witnessed her faith and his companions shed tears of joy, she bade them farewell and joined her Lord. She, a drop in the sea of illusion, returned to the true ocean and the shaykh came to Baghdad and stretched his neck in humbleness under the feet of Ḥaḍrat ʿAbdul-Qādir.

As Ḥaḍrat ʿAbdul-Qādir's influence spread to all comers of the world, many of his disciples obtained important positions and many rulers of men became his disciples. In accordance with their abilities, inner qualities and spiritual levels, he charged many of his followers to act as his deputies. Some he made spiritual teachers and others jurists. Some he even appointed as governors and wielders of worldly power.

There was a dervish who had been with Ḥaḍrat ʿAbdul-Qādir for forty years, who had entered his service and had made all efforts to please him. He would see other disciples much younger than he, who spent much less time than he did with the shaykh, delegated by the shaykh to receive important posts. One day he came to Ḥaḍrat ʿAbdul-Qādir and made a request. He had served him for so many years and now he was getting old. Why could he not also receive an important and lofty post like some of the others?

As he was speaking, a group of emissaries from India arrived. They wished Ḥaḍrat ʿAbdul-Qādir to appoint a maharajah to their kingdom. The shaykh looked at his dervish and said, 'Would you like this post? Do you feel that you are qualified?' The dervish was overjoyed.

After the emissaries left, the shaykh said to the dervish, 'If you feel qualified to serve in my name I will appoint you to that kingdom in India. I have a condition. You must promise to give me half of all the profit and goods you will receive during your reign.' The dervish readily accepted.

This dervish was a cook at Ḥaḍrat ʿAbdul-Qādir's school. That day a dessert was being prepared which had to be stirred continuously. After his talk with the shaykh he returned to the kitchen to stir the heavy dessert in a giant cauldron with a wooden spoon. While he was engaged in this he was called to accompany the emissaries to India as their king, and he left.

The dervish became a maharajah. He gathered enormous wealth, built many palaces for himself, married and had a son. He forgot all about his shaykh and about his promise.

Then one day he received a message that Shaykh ʿAbdul-Qādir was coming to visit his kingdom. He prepared to receive him with great pomp. After lavish ceremonies, processions, and feasts, they were left alone to speak. The shaykh reminded the maharajah of their agreement: he was to receive half of all that he had accumulated during his reign. The maharajah was displeased at being reminded of his promise but nevertheless avowed that by the following day he would prepare an account of all he possessed and would offer half to the shaykh.

His ambition and his hunger for wealth—which had increased many times, the more wealth he acquired—did not permit him to account truthfully for his possessions. The next day he brought a list and presented it to the shaykh. Although it enumerated many palaces and many treasures it represented only a fraction of what he actually owned.

Shaykh ʿAbdul-Qādir seemed to be satisfied with his share. Then he spoke. 'I hear that you also have a son.'

The maharajah responded, 'Yes, unfortunately only one. If I had two I would gladly give you one.'

'Nonetheless, bring the child,' the shaykh returned. 'We can always share him.' The boy was brought into their presence. The shaykh unsheathed his sharp sword and held it over the child's head. 'You will have half and I will have half!' he declared.

The father, horrified, pulled out his dagger and with his two hands plunged it into the heart of the shaykh.

He blinked his eyes: as he opened them he found himself at the edge of the cauldron of dessert, plunging the wooden spoon into it. Ḥaḍrat ʿAbdul-Qādir looked at him and said, 'As you see, you are not yet ready to be my representative. You have not yet given everything, including yourself, to me.'

He himself had given all of himself to Allah. His nights passed with little or no sleep in secluded prayer and meditation. He spent his days like a true follower of the Prophet in the service of humanity. Three times a week he would deliver public sermons to thousands of people. Every day in the morning and the afternoon he gave lessons in Qur'ānic commentary, Prophetic traditions, theology, religious law and Sufism. He spent the time after the midday prayer giving advice and consultation to people, whether beggars or kings, who would come from all parts of the world. Before sunset prayers, rain or shine, he took to the streets to distribute bread among the poor. As he spent all his days in fasting he would eat only once a day, after the sunset prayer, and never alone. His servants would stand at his door asking passers-by if they were hungry, so that they could share his table.

He died on Saturday the eighth day of II Rabī' in 561 A.H., 1166 C.E, at the age of 91. His blessed tomb, at the madrasa of Bāb al-Daraja in Baghdad, has become an important place of visitation for Sufis and all Muslims.

When he contracted the illness from which he died his son ʿAbdul-ʿAzīz saw that he was suffering great pain, tossing and turning in bed. 'Do not worry about me,' he said to his son. 'I am being turned over and over again in the knowledge of Allah.'

When his son ʿAbdul-Jabbār asked him where it hurt him he said, 'All of me aches except for my heart. There is no pain in it, for it is with Allah.'

His son ʿAbdul-Wahhāb said to him, 'Give me some last advice upon which to act after you have left this world.'

He said, 'Fear Allah and none other. Hope from Allah and entrust all your needs to Him; hope and want nothing from anyone except Him. Rely on Allah and on none other. Unite with Him, unite with Him, unite with Him.'

Before he left this world he looked around and said to the people present, 'Others whom you do not see have come to me. Make room and show courtesy to them! I am the core without the shell. You see me with you, while I am with someone else. It is best that you leave me now.' Then he said, 'O angel of death, I do not fear you nor do I fear anything except Him Who has befriended me and has been generous to me!'

At the last moment he raised his hands and said, 'There is no god but Allah and Muḥammad is His Prophet. Glory be to Allah, the Exalted, the Ever-living, glory be to Him, the All-Powerful, Who overpowers His servants by death.'

Then he gave a loud cry and said, 'Allah, Allah, Allah!' and his blessed soul left his body.

May Allah's pleasure be upon his soul and may his spirit intercede for this faqīr, the writer of these words, and for those who read them.

يا حضرت شيخ سيد عبد القادر الكيلاني

An Address to the Reader

(*From a letter by* Ḥaḍrat ʿAbdul-Qādir al-Jīlānī)

DEAR FRIEND, Your heart is a polished mirror. You must wipe it clean of the veil of dust which has gathered upon it, because it is destined to reflect the light of divine secrets.

When the light from *Allah* (Who) is *the light of the heavens and the earth...* begins to shine upon the regions of your heart, the lamp of the heart will be lit. The lamp of the heart is *in a glass, the glass is as it were a brightly shining star...* Then within that heart, the lightning-shaft of divine discoveries strikes. This lightning-shaft will emanate from the thunderclouds of meaning *neither of the East nor of the West, lit from a blessed olive tree...* and throw light upon the tree of discovery, so pure, so transparent that it *sheds light though fire does not touch it.*[1] Then the lamp of wisdom is lit by itself. How can it remain unlit when the light of Allah's secrets shines over it?

If only the light of divine secrets shines upon it, the night sky of secrets is lit with thousands of stars... *and by the stars* (you) *find* (your) *way...*[2] It is not the stars that guide us but the divine light. For Allah has... *decked the lower heaven with beauty* (in) *the stars.*[3] If only the lamp of divine secrets be kindled in your inner self the rest will come, either all at once or little by little. Some you already know, some we will tell you here. Read, listen, try to understand. The dark skies of unconsciousness will be lit by divine presence and the peace and beauty of the full moon, which will rise from the horizon shedding *light upon light*,[4] ever rising in the sky, passing through its appointed stages as Allah has... ordained for it Mansions,[5] until it shines in glory in the centre of the sky, dispersing the darkness of heedlessness. (I swear) *by the night when it is still*[6]... *By the glorious morning light*...[7] your night of unconsciousness will see the brightness of the day. Then you will inhale the perfume of remembrance and *repent in the early hours of the morning*[8] of unconsciousness and regret your life spent in sleep. You will hear the songs of the morning nightingales and you will hear them say

> *They were in the habit of sleeping but little by night, and in the hours of early dawn they* (were found) *praying for forgiveness.*[9]

> *Allah guides to His light whom He pleases.*[10]

Then you will see from the horizon of Divine Reason the sun of inner knowledge rising. It is your private sun, for you are the one *whom Allah guides* and are *on the right path* and not the one *He leaves in error.*[11] And you will understand the secret that

> *It is not given to the sun to catch up with the moon, nor can the night outstrip the day. Each swims along in* (its appointed) *orbit.*[12]

Finally, the knot will be untied in accordance with *the parables which Allah sets forth for men, and Allah is the Knower of all things*,[13] and the veils will lift and shells will shatter, revealing the fine beneath the coarse; the truth will uncover her face.

All this will begin when the mirror of your heart is cleansed. The light of the divine secrets will fall upon it if you are willing and ask for Him, from Him, with Him.

NOTES

[1]All the above are quoted from the Verse of Light (Sūra Nūr, 35).
[2]Sūra Naḥl, 16.
[3]Sūra Ṣāffāt, 6.

[4] Sūra Nūr, 35.
[5] Sūra Yā Sīn, 39.
[6] Sūra Ḍuḥā, 2.
[7] Sūra Ḍuḥā, 1.
[8] Sūra Āl ʿImrān, 17.
[9] Sūra Dhāriyāt, 17–18.
[10] Sūra Nūr, 35.
[11] Sūra Aʿrāf, 178.
[12] Sūra Yā Sīn, 40.
[13] Sūra Nūr, 35.

یا حضرت پیر شیخ سلطان سید عبد القادر گیلانی
١٣١٩

The Secret of Secrets

بسم الله الرحمن الرحيم

INTRODUCTION

All praise is due to Allah, as He is a munificent, gracious and compassionate Lord, Who has gathered all knowledge in His Essence and Who is the Creator of all knowledge for eternity. The cause, the reason of all existence is from His existence. All praise is due to Allah, as He has sent the Glorious Qur'ān that bears in its essence the reason for its revelation, which is to remind men of Allah; He sent it to the guide who leads men on the path of truth with the mightiest of all religions. All peace and blessings be upon His beloved prophet Muḥammad, who was not taught by man, but by Him. He is His last prophet, the last link in the chain of prophethood who was brought to a world gone astray, the most honoured among His prophets, honoured by the most honoured of divine books. His progeny are guides for seekers, his companions were chosen among the good and benevolent. May abundant peace and blessings be upon their souls.

Certainly the most honourable of valuable things, the highest, the priceless jewel, the most profitable object of trade among men, is knowledge. Only with wisdom can we attain the unity of Allah, Lord of all the universes. Only with wisdom can we understand and follow His messengers and His prophets, peace and blessings be upon them. The men of knowledge, the wise men, are the pure servants of Allah whom He has chosen to receive divine messages. He has preferred them to other men by virtue of the grace He has poured upon them. They are the heirs of His prophets, their deputies, whom His messengers chose to be masters of men. They are connected to His prophets with the finest of feeling and with the wisest of intelligence.

Allah Most High praises the possessors of wisdom in His Qur'ān:

> *Then We have given the Book as an inheritance to those whom We have chosen from among Our servants: So some of them are those who wrong themselves and some of them are those who take the middle course* [whose errors and good deeds are equal], *and some of them are those who are foremost in deeds of goodness by Allah's will. That is the greatest grace.* (Sūra Fāṭir, 32)

Then our Master, the Prophet of Allah (God bless him and grant him peace) praises them, saying, 'The holders of wisdom are the heirs of the prophets. The inhabitants of the heavens love them, and upon this earth even the fishes in the seas praise them until Doomsday.' In another verse, Allah Most High credits the men of knowledge, describing them thus:

> *Certainly those of His servants who are possessed of knowledge fear Him.* (Sūra Fāṭir, 28)

Our Master the Prophet ﷺ, says, 'On the day of the Last Judgment Allah will gather men together, then separate the wise men from among them, and say to them, "O people of knowledge, I gave you My knowledge because I know you. I did not give you wisdom to punish you on this day. Enter My Paradise; I have forgiven you".'

All praise belongs to Allah, Lord of the universes, for He has given high stations to His devout servants to protect them from sin and to spare them punishment. He has blessed the wise by drawing near to them.

Some of our students asked us to prepare a book which would suffice them. In compliance with their wish and their need we have prepared this short book: may it heal and satisfy them and others. We named this book *Sirr al-asrār fī mā yaḥtāju ilayhi al-abrār*—'The Secret of Secrets of which the Righteous are in Need.' In this work the realities within our faith and our path are divulged. Everyone is in need of them.

In presenting this work we have divided it into twenty-four chapters because there are twenty-four letters in the sacred confession of Unity *Lā ilāha illā Llāh, Muḥammadun rasūlu Llāh* ('There is no god but Allah; Muḥammad is the Messenger of Allah'), and there are twenty-four hours in a day and a night.

ON THE BEGINNING OF CREATION

May Allah accord you success in acts which please Him and meet with His approval.

Think, impress upon your mind and understand what I say.

Allah Most High first created, from the divine light of His own Beauty, the light of Muḥammad ﷺ. He declares this in a divine tradition related from Him by the Prophet ﷺ:

> I have created the soul of Muḥammad from the light of my Manifestation (*wajh*).

This is declared by our Master the Messenger of Allah in his words, 'Allah first created my soul. He first created it as a divine light;' 'Allah created the Pen first;' 'Allah first created the Intellect.' What is meant by all that is mentioned as having been created first is the creation of the truth of Muḥammad, the hidden reality of Muḥammad ﷺ. He is also [like his Lord] called by many beautiful names. He is called *Nūr*, the Divine Light, because he was purified of the darkness hidden under the attribute of the might and wrath (*jalāl*) of Allah. Allah Most High says in His Holy Qur'ān:

> *There has come to you from Allah a light and a perspicuous Book.* (Sūra Mā'idah, 15)

He is called the Total Intellect (*ʿaql al-kull*) because he saw and understood everything. He is called the Pen (*al-qalam*) because he spread wisdom and knowledge, and he poured knowledge into the realm of letters.

The soul of Muḥammad is the essence of all beings, the beginning and the reality of the universe. He indicates this with the words, 'I am from Allah and the believers are from me'. Allah Most High created all souls from his soul in the realm of the first created beings, in the best of forms. 'Muḥammad' is the name of all humanity in the realm of souls (*'ālam al-arwāḥ*). He is the source, the home of each and every thing.

Four thousand years after the creation of the light of Muḥammad, Allah created the Heavenly Throne (*ʿarsh*) from the light of the eye of Muḥammad. He created the rest of creation from the Heavenly Throne. Then He sent the souls to descend to the lowest levels of creation, to the realm of this material world, to the realm of matter and bodies. *Then We make him descend to the lowest of the low.* (Sūra Tīn, 5). He sent that light from where it was created, from the Ultimate Realm (*'ālam al-lāhūt*)—which is the realm of the manifestation of Allah's Essence, of unity, of absolute being—to the realm of the divine Names, the manifestation of the divine attributes, the realm of the causal intelligence of the Total Soul. There He dressed the souls in robes of light. These souls are called 'sultan-souls'. Clothed in light they descended to the realm of the angels. There He clothed them with the brilliant robes of angels, there they were called 'spiritual souls'. Then He caused them to descend to the world of matter, of water and fire, earth and ether, and they became human souls. Then from this world He created the bodies of flesh.

> *From it We created you and into it We shall return you, and from it raise you a second time.* (Sūra Ṭā Hā, 55)

After these stages, Allah ordered the souls to enter into their bodies, and by His will they entered.

So when I have made him complete and breathed into him of My Soul... (Sūra Ṣād, 72)

A time came when these souls started binding themselves to the flesh and forgot their source and their covenant. They forgot that when Allah created them in the realm of souls He had asked them *Am I not your Lord?* and they had answered, *Indeed!* They forgot their promise, they forgot their source, their way to return home; but Allah is merciful, the source of all help and security for His creation. He had mercy upon them, so He sent divine books and messengers to them to remind them of their origin.

> *And certainly We sent Moses with Our messages* [saying]: *Bring forth the people from darkness into light, and remind them of the days of Allah...* (Sūra Ibrāhīm, 5)

That is, 'Remind the souls of the days when they were in union with Allah.'

Many messengers have come to this world, fulfilled their duties, and passed away. The purpose of all was to bring men the message and awaken people to heedfulness. But people who remembered Him, who turned toward Him, people who wished to return to their divine origin, people who arrived at their origin, became fewer and fewer with time.

The prophets kept coming and the divine message continued until there appeared the great spirit of Muḥammad ﷺ, the last of the messengers who saved people from distraction. Allah Most High sent him to open the eyes of the hearts of the heedless. His purpose was to awaken them from the sleep of unconsciousness and to unite them with the Eternal Beauty, with the Cause, with the Essence of Allah. Allah says in His Holy Qur'ān:

> *Say: This is my way. I call to Allah with the certainty of insight—I and those who follow me...* (Sūra Yūsuf, 108)

to indicate the path of our Master the Prophet ﷺ.

The Messenger of Allah, to indicate our goal to us, says, 'My companions are like the stars in the sky. Whichever of them you follow, you will find the true path.'

This insight comes from the eye of the soul. This eye opens in the heart's heart of those who are close to Allah, who are Allah's friends. All the knowledge in the material world will not provide this insight: one needs a knowledge that comes from the hidden realms, a knowledge which overflows from divine consciousness: *... whom We had taught knowledge from Our Divine Presence.* (Sūra Kahf, 65)

What is necessary for man is to find those who have insight, whose eyes of the heart are open, and to be inspired by them. Such a teacher who inculcates knowledge into one has to be close to Allah and able to see into the Ultimate Realm.

O children of Adam, brothers and sisters, wake up, repent, for through repentance you will be asking your Lord for His wisdom. Make an effort and strive! Allah commands you:

> *And hasten to forgiveness from your Lord, and a Garden as wide as the heavens and the earth; it is prepared for the righteous* [who fear and love Allah]:
>
> *Those who spend in ease as well as in adversity and those who restrain* [their] *anger and pardon men. And Allah loves the doers of good* [to others]. (Sūra Āl 'Imrān, 133–34)

Enter the path, join the spiritual caravan to return to your Lord. Soon the road will become impassable, and no travelling companion will be left. We did not come to this base, mined world to rest; we were not sent here to eat, drink and defecate. The spirit of our Master, the Prophet of Allah, is watching you. He is pained, seeing your state. He knew what would come when he said, 'My pain is for my beloved people who will come in later times'.

Whatever comes to us comes in one of two forms, either evident or hidden: evident in the form of the precepts of the religion or hidden in the form of wisdom. Allah Most High orders us to render our exterior being harmonious by following the religious precepts and to put our inner being in order through acquiring wisdom. When the outer and the inner become one and wisdom and religion unite, one reaches the level of truth, like the fruit tree that first produces leaves, then buds, and then flowers that become fruit.

He has made two seas to flow freely—they meet: Between them is a barrier that they cannot pass. (Sūra Raḥmān, 19–20)

The two must become one. Truth cannot be attained only through the tangible knowledge of the senses, of the material universe. One cannot in that way reach the goal, which is the origin, the Essence. True worship necessitates both religion and wisdom. Allah Most High says about worship:

And I have not created the jinn and men except that they should worship Me. (Sūra Dhāriyāt, 56)

In other words, 'they are created so that they might know Me.' When one does not know Him, how can one truly praise Him, ask His help and serve Him?

The wisdom which one needs in order to know Him can only be attained by lifting the black curtain covering the mirror of one's heart, cleaning that mirror and shining it. Then the hidden treasures of divine beauty may begin reflecting in the secret of the heart's mirror.

Allah Most High, speaking through His beloved Prophet, says: 'I was a hidden treasure, I willed to be known, therefore I created Creation.' Consequently, the divine purpose in the creation of man is for him to acquire wisdom, to know his Lord.

There are two levels of divine wisdom. One is to know Allah's attributes and manifestations and the other is to know Allah's Essence. In knowing Allah's attributes the material man tastes both this world and the hereafter. But the wisdom which leads to the knowledge of the Essence of Allah is in the holy spirit in man knowing the mysteries of the hereafter. Allah confirms this, saying: . . . *and We strengthened him* [Jesus] *with the holy spirit. . .* (Sūra Baqara, 87). Those who know the Essence of Allah find this power through the holy spirit that has been given to them.

Both of these knowledges are obtained by a wisdom that must have two aspects: the inner spiritual wisdom and the outer knowledge of manifest things. One is in need of both to attain the good. The Prophet of Allah ﷺ explains them thus: 'Knowledge is of two parts. One is in man's tongue, which is a proof of Allah's existence. The other is in man's heart. This is what is necessary for the realization of our hopes.'

Man is first in need of religious knowledge. This is the education in which one is taught the exterior manifestation of Allah's Essence reflected in this world of attributes and names. After one becomes accomplished in this, it is the turn of the inner education in the secrets whereby one enters into the realms of divine wisdom and comes to know the truth. At the first stage one must leave everything that is not in accordance with religious precepts. In fact, errors—mistakes in good behaviour and character—must be eliminated, as the Sufis require. To achieve this one must practice doing things against the wishes of one's ego, acts which are difficult for the desires of the flesh to accept. But in these efforts one must be attentive, so that they are not made for others to see and hear about. One must do these things for Allah's sake, seeking only His pleasure. Allah says:

> *. . . so whoever hopes to meet his Lord, he should do good deeds and associate none other in the service of his Lord.* (Sūra Kahf, 110)

The realm described as the realm of wisdom is the first-created Ultimate Realm. That realm is the origin, the home to which one aspires to return. That is where the holy spirit was created. What is meant by the holy spirit is the human spirit. It was created in the best of forms.

That truth has been planted in the centre of the heart as Allah's trust, entrusted to you for safekeeping. It becomes manifest with true repentance and with the true effort to learn religion. Its beauty shines on the surface when one remembers Allah continuously, repeating the Confession of Unity *Lā ilāha illā Llāh*—'There is no god but Allah'. At the first stage one recites the Confession of Unity with one's tongue; then when the heart becomes alive one recites internally with the heart.

The Sufis refer to the spiritual states by the name *ṭifl*, 'babe', because that baby is born in the heart and is reared and grows there. The heart, like a mother, gives birth, suckles, feeds, rears the child of the heart. As worldly sciences are taught to children, the child of the heart is taught the inner wisdom. As an ordinary child is not yet soiled with worldly sins, the child of the heart is pure, free from heedlessness, egotism and doubt. The purity of a child appears often as physical beauty; in the world of dreams the purity of the heart's child appears in the shape of angels. One hopes to enter Paradise as a reward for good deeds, but gifts of Paradise come here through the hands of the child of the heart.

> *In Gardens of bliss. . . round about them will go youths never altering in age.* (Sūra Wāqi'a, 12–17)
>
> *And round them go boys of theirs, as if they were hidden pearls.* (Sūra Ṭūr, 24)

These are the children of the heart, the inspired states of the Sufis, called 'children' for their beauty and purity. Yet they are beauty and purity personified in flesh, in the shape of human beings. Due to their sweet and gentle nature they are the children of the heart, yet is he the true man who is able to change the appearance of creation because he is connected to the Creator. He is the true representative of humanity. According to him there is no matter, neither does he consider himself matter. There is no veil, no hindrance, between his being and the Essence of Allah.

Our Master the Prophet ﷺ explains this state, 'I have a time with Allah. At that moment nothing can come between us, neither the angel closest to Him nor a prophet.' The 'prophet' who cannot enter between our Master and Allah is the material, temporal existence of the Prophet himself. The angel closest to Allah is the divine Light of Muḥammad, the first creation. In that inspired state he is so close to his Lord that neither his material existence nor even his soul can come between them. The Prophet ﷺ describes the time of that inspired state, saying, 'There is a paradise of Allah where there are no palaces, nor gardens, nor rivers of honey and milk, a paradise where one gazes only at the divine countenance.' Allah confirms this: [Some] *faces that day will be bright, looking to their Lord*, (Sūra Qiyāma, 22–23) and the Prophet ﷺ says, 'On that day you will see your Lord as clear as the full moon.' But this is a state that, if any created being, even an angel, should approach, his material being would burn to ashes. Allah speaks through His Prophet ﷺ:

> *If I parted the veils of my attribute of Might a mere crack, all would burn as far as My eye can see.*

The archangel Gabriel عليه السلام, who accompanied the Prophet ﷺ in his Ascension to the seventh heaven, said that if he took one step further he would be set aflame.

CHAPTER ONE

Man's Return Home to the Original Source

MAN is considered from two points of view: his material being and his spiritual being. In the appearance of material being everyone is more or less equal. Therefore, in this respect, one may apply to humanity general laws. In his spiritual being, hidden behind his appearance, each person is different. Therefore special private laws apply to him.

Man, in accordance with general laws, by following certain steps can return to his origin. To take these steps, he follows the evident ordinances of our religion as a guide; following them, he advances. Rising from level to level he may reach the stage of the spiritual path, passing into the realm of wisdom. That is a very high state. The Prophet ﷺ praises this state, saying, 'There is a state in which all and everything is gathered—and it is the divine wisdom.'

To reach that level, one first has to abandon false appearances and the hypocrisy of doing things so that others might see or hear. Then one must set for oneself three goals. These three goals are actually three paradises. The first is called *Ma'wā*—the paradise of the security of home. That is the earthly paradise. The second is called *Naʿīm*—the garden of the delight of Allah's grace upon His creatures, which is the paradise within the angelic realm. The third is called *Firdaws*—the heavenly paradise. That is the paradise in the realm of the unity of the causal mind, home of the souls, of the divine Names and attributes. These are the rewards, the beauties of Allah which the material man will taste in his efforts in the three successive stages of knowledge: efforts in following the religious precepts (*sharīʿa*); efforts in eliminating the multiplicity in himself, fighting the cause of this multiplicity which is his ego, in order to reach the state of unity and come close to his Creator (*ṭarīqa*); and finally, in his efforts to reach the state of divine wisdom (*maʿrifa*) whereby he will come to know his Lord.

The Prophet ﷺ at the conclusion of the previously mentioned tradition, 'There is a state in which all and everything is gathered and it is the divine wisdom,' says: 'With it one learns the truth, which gathers within itself all causes and all good. Then one must act upon this truth. One must also know falsehood and act upon It, abandoning all of it.' And he says, 'O Lord, show us the truth and make it our lot to follow it, and teach us that which is false and make it easy for us to avoid it.' And, 'He who knows his self and opposes its wrong desires truly, comes to know his Lord, and follows His wishes.'

These are the general rules which apply to the material being of man. Then there is the spiritual being of man, or the spiritual man, who is called the pure man. His goal is total closeness to Allah. The only way to this end is the knowledge of truth (*ḥaqīqa*). In the first-created realm of the absolute being of oneness, this knowledge is called Unity.

One may hope to reach the goal of this path in this worldly life. In that state there is no difference between being awake and being asleep, since in sleep the soul may find occasion to escape to its true home, the realm of the souls, and come back and bring news. This we call the true dream. This event can be partial, as in the case of dreams; it can also be total, as in the case of the Ascension of the Prophet ﷺ. Allah confirms this:

> *Allah takes* (men's) *souls at the time of their death, and those that die not, during their sleep. Then He withholds those on whom He bas passed the decree of death, and sends the others back till an appointed*

> *term. Surely there are signs in this for a people who reflect.* (Sūra Zumar, 42)

The Prophet ﷺ indicates this state by saying, 'The sleep of the wise is more worthy than the worship of the ignorant.' The wise are those who have acquired the knowledge of truth that has no letters, no sound. That knowledge is received through the continuous repetition of the divine Name of Unity with the secret tongue. The wise are those whose core is turned into divine light by the light of unity.

Allah speaks through His Prophet ﷺ and says:

> Man is My secret and I am his secret. The inner knowledge of the spiritual essence *('ilm al-bāṭin)* is a secret of My secrets. Only I put this into the heart of My good servant, and none may know his state other than Me.

and:

> I am as My servant knows Me. When he seeks Me and remembers Me, I am with him. If he seeks me inwardly, I seek him with My Essence. If he remembers and mentions Me in good company, I remember and declare him as My good servant in better company.

In all that is said here, the only way to satisfy one's wish is meditation—that means of knowledge which the common man uses so seldom. Yet the Prophet of Allah ﷺ said, 'A moment's reflection is worth more than a year of worship'. 'A moment's reflection is worth more than seventy years of worship'. 'A moment's reflection is worth more than a thousand years of worship.'

The value of every action is hidden in the essence of truth. The act of a moment's meditation here appears to have three different values:

Whoever contemplates an affair and seeks its cause finds that each of its parts has many parts of its own, and finds that each of these is the cause of many other things. This is a contemplation that is worth a year's worship.

Whoever contemplates his devotions and seeks the cause and reason and comes to know it, his meditation is worth seventy years of worship.

Whoever contemplates the divine wisdom with a strong wish to know Allah Most High, his meditation is worth a thousand years of worship, for this is the true knowledge.

True knowledge is the state of unity. The wise lover unites with his Beloved. From this material realm, flying with spiritual wings he soars to the realm of attainment, for the devout walk to Paradise while the wise fly to the realms close to their Lord.

Lovers have eyes in their hearts.
They see, while others are staring blind.
Such wings they have, not of flesh and blood.
They fly towards angels, their Lord to find!

This flight occurs in the inner world of the wise. They receive the honour of being called true men, the beloved ones of Allah, His intimates, His brides. The saint Bāyazīd al-Bisṭāmī, may Allah sanctity his secret, says, 'The holders of wisdom are the brides of Allah Most High.' Others as well describe them by saying that those who come close to Allah become the brides of Allah.

Only the loving possessors of brides know them intimately. These wise servants who become intimates of Allah, though beautiful, are covered by the appearance of ordinary men. Allah speaks through His Prophet ﷺ, saying: 'My intimates are hidden under My domes. None can recognize them but Me.' The domes under which Allah hides His friends are their undistinguished, ordinary appearances. When one looks at a bride covered by her wedding veil, what can one see but the veil?

Yaḥyā ibn Mu'ādh al-Rāzī, may Allah sanctify his secret, says, 'The beloved of Allah are the perfume of Allah upon this world, but only the true, sincere believers have noses to smell them.' They smell that beautiful perfume; they follow that smell. That perfume creates a yearning in their hearts for their Lord. Each in his own way increases his pace, his efforts, his devotion. The degree of his yearning, his wish and the speed of his pace are in proportion to his lightness, to his having shed the weight of his worldly self. For the more one takes off the coarse clothing of this world, the more one feels the warmth of one's Creator and the closer to the surface inner being comes. Closeness to the truth is in relation to the amount of false materially one has thrown away. In giving away one's multiple aspects one comes closer to the only truth.

The intimate of Allah is he who has brought himself to nothingness. Only then can he see the existence of the truth. There is no will left in him to choose. There is no 'I' left other than the only existence, which is the truth. Although all manner of miracles have come through him to prove this state, he has nothing to do with them. In his state there is no disclosure of secrets, because divulging the secret of divinity is infidelity.

In a book called *Mirṣād* it is written, 'All men through whom miracles appear are veiled from and unconcerned about their states. For them, the times when miracles appear are considered to be like the periods of menstruation for women. Saints who are intimate with Allah have to travel through at least a thousand stages, the first of which is the door of miracles. Only those who are able to pass through this door unharmed can reach the other stages. If they become involved, they will get nowhere.'

CHAPTER TWO

The Descent of Man to the Lowest of the Low

Allah Most High created the holy spirit as the most perfect creation in the first-created realm of the absolute being of His Essence; then He willed to send it to lower realms. His reason in that was to teach the holy spirit to seek the way back to the truth on the level of the All-Powerful, to seek its previous closeness and intimacy with Allah. He sent the holy spirit to the station of His messengers and saints and lovers and friends. On its way Allah sent it first to the realm of the Causal Mind, of unity, of the Total Soul, the realm of His divine Names and attributes, the realm of the truth of Muḥammad ﷺ. The holy spirit had with it the seed of unity. As it passed through this realm it was given the clothing of divine light and was named the sultan-soul. As it passed through the realm of angels, which is the medium of dreams, it received the name 'moving soul'. When it finally descended to this world of matter it was dressed in the clothing of flesh that Allah created to fit its being. It was clothed with coarse matter in order to save this world, because the material world, if it had direct contact with the holy spirit, would burn to ashes. In relation to this world, it came to be known as life, the human soul.

The purpose of the spirit's coming to this lowest of created realms is that it should seek to return to its previous closeness while in its actual form of flesh and bone: that it should come to this realm of coarse matter and, by means of the heart which is inside this corpse, plant the seed of unity and grow the tree of unity therein. (The roots of that tree are where they have always been; its branches fill the void of bliss, and there, for the pleasure of Allah, bear the fruits of unity.) Then in the earth of the heart the spirit planted the seed of religion and wished to grow the tree of religion, in order to obtain fruits, each of which would raise it to levels closer to Allah.

Allah made bodies for the souls to enter, and for these souls, each of which has a different name, He built fitting spaces within the bodies. He placed the human soul, the soul of life, between the flesh and the blood. He placed the holy spirit within the centre of the heart, where he built a space of fine matter to keep that secret between Allah and His servant. These souls are in different parts of the body, with different duties, with different businesses; each, as if by buying and selling different goods, obtains different benefits. Their business always brings them plenty in the form of Allah's bounty and blessings.

> *Out of what We have provided for them, secretly and openly,* (they) *hope for commerce that will never fail.* (Sūra Fāṭir, 29)

It befits every human being to know his business within this universe of his own existence, and to understand its purpose. He must understand that he cannot change whatever is judged right for him and hung around his neck. Of the one who wishes to change his lot, who is tied to this world and ambitious for it, Allah asks:

> *Knows he not when that which is in the graves is raised, and that which is in the breasts is made manifest?* (Sūra ʿĀdiyāt, 9–10)

> *And We have made every man's actions to cling to his neck. . .* (Sūra Banī Isrā'īl, 13)

CHAPTER THREE

The Places of the Souls within the Body

THE place of the human soul, the soul of life, within the body is the breast. That place is connected to the senses. Its business is religion; its work is to follow Allah's precepts. With these precepts Allah keeps the visible world in harmony and order. That soul, acting upon the obligations set by Allah, does not claim its actions as its own, for it is not separate from Allah, its actions are from Allah: there is no separation between it and Allah in its actions and devotions.

> *To meet his Lord let him work righteousness and in the worship of his Lord admit no one as partner.* (Sūra Kahf, 110)

Allah is One and He loves that which is united and one. He wants all worship and all righteous acts, which He considers as devotion, to belong to Himself alone. Therefore a man should not take other people's approval or rejection into consideration in his actions; neither should his actions be for worldly benefit. They should be solely for Allah's sake. Inspired states such as seeing in this visible world the proof of Allah's existence—manifestation of His attributes, the unity within the multiplicity, the truth behind appearances—and closeness to one's Creator, are the rewards for these selfless righteous acts and devotions. Yet all these still belong to this world of matter, from the ground under one's feet up to the heavens. So also to this world belong the miracles that may appear through one: walking on water, flying in the air, travelling great distances in a very short time, hearing sounds, seeing images from faraway places, knowing hidden thoughts. As a reward for righteous actions, one may also hope to find rewards in the hereafter—palaces of Paradise, young manservants, eternal virgins as companions, milk, honey, wine and all the other benefits of Paradise. Yet all these are bounties of the first level of Paradise, the earthly paradise.

The place of the 'moving soul' is in the heart; its business is with the knowledge of the spiritual path. Its work deals with the first four of the Beautiful Names of the Essence of Allah. As in the rest of the twelve Names of the Essence, these four Names have neither sound nor letters—thus they cannot be pronounced. Allah Most High indicates this:

> *Say: Call on Allah or call on the Beneficent. By whatever* (name) *you call on Him, He has the Most Beautiful Names.* (Sūra Banī Isrā'īl, 110)

> *And Allah's are the Most Beautiful Names, so call on Him thereby...* (Sūra A'rāf, 180)

Allah's very words point to what should be man's principal occupation: to know the divine Names. This is the knowledge of one's inner being. If one obtained that knowledge, one would reach the level of divine wisdom. That is where the knowledge of the Name of Unity is complete.

Our Master the Prophet ﷺ says of the divine Names, 'Allah Most High has ninety-nine Names. Whoever learns them enters Paradise'. He also says, 'Knowledge is one. Then men of knowledge made it a thousand.' This means that the Name which belongs to the Essence is only one; it is reflected as a thousand attributes in those who receive it.

The twelve divine Names are within the origin of the Confession of Unity, *Lā ilāha illā Llāh*, 'There is no god but Allah'. Each of them is in one of the twelve letters in this phrase. Allah Most High has given an individual Name to each letter in the development of the heart. Each of the four realms through which the soul passes also has three different Names. Allah Most High in this way holds the hearts of the lovers firmly in love. He says:

> *Allah will establish in strength* (the hearts) *of those who believe with the word that stands firm in this world and in the Hereafter.* (Sūra Ibrāhīm, 27)

Then He gives them the gift of His intimacy. He sets the tree of unity in their hearts, that tree whose roots descend to the seventh Level beneath us and whose branches spread to the seven heavens above us up to the divine Throne and perhaps still higher. Allah says:

> *Seest thou not how Allah sets forth a parable of a good word as a good tree, whose root is firm and whose branches are high?* (Sūra Ibrāhīm, 24)

The place of the 'moving soul' is within the life of the heart. The angelic realm is constantly within its view. It can see the paradises of that realm, its inhabitants, its light, and all the angels within it. The speech of the 'moving soul' is the speech of the inner world, without words, without sound. Its thoughts constantly concern the secrets of the hidden meanings. Its place in the Hereafter, upon its return, is the paradise of *Na'īm,* the garden of the delights of Allah's grace.

The place of the sultan-soul, where it reigns, is the centre of the heart, the heart of the heart. The business of this soul is divine wisdom. Its work is to know all of divine knowledge, which is the medium of true devotion recited in the language of the heart. The Prophet ﷺ explains this. 'Knowledge is in two sections. One is in man's tongue, which is the confirmation of Allah's existence. The other is in man's heart. That is the one necessary for the realization of man's goal.' The truly beneficial knowledge is only within the framework of the heart's activity. As the Prophet ﷺ says, 'The Holy Qur'ān has an outer meaning and an inner meaning.' Allah Most

High revealed the Holy Qur'ān in ten layers of hidden meaning. Each successive meaning is more beneficial than the one before, because it is closer to the source of truth. The twelve divine Names belonging to the Essence of Allah are like the twelve fountains which gushed forth from the stone when the prophet Moses (peace be upon him) hit it with his staff.

> *And when Moses prayed for water for his people, We said: Strike it with thy staff. So there flowed from it twelve springs. Each tribe knew its drinking place. . .* (Sūra Baqara, 60)

The outer knowledge of appearances is like rainwater, which comes and goes, while the inner knowledge is like a fountain whose source never dries up. Allah says:

> *And a sign to them is the dead earth: We give life to it and bring forth from it grain so they eat of it.* (Sūra Yā Sīn, 33)

Allah has created a grain, a seed in the skies. That seed became the strength of the animal in man. And He has created a seed in the realm of the souls (*ʿālam al-anfus*): that is the source of strength, the food of the soul. That grain is watered by the source of wisdom. As the Prophet says, 'If someone spends forty days in sincerity and purity, the source of wisdom will gush from his heart to his tongue.'

The benefit of the sultan-soul is the rapture and love that it feels watching the manifestation of Allah's beauty, grace, and perfection. As Allah confirms:

> *One Mighty in Power has taught him,*
> *The Lord of Strength. So he attained perfection,*
> *And he is in the highest part of the horizon.*
> *Then he drew near, drew yet nearer,*
> *So that he was the measure of two bows or closer still*
> *So He revealed to His servant what He revealed.*
> *The heart was not untrue in seeing what he saw.*
>
> (Sūra Najm, 5–11)

The Prophet ﷺ describes this state in another way: 'The faithful is the mirror of the faithful'. In this phrase, the first 'faithful' is the heart of the perfect believer, and the second 'faithful', which is reflected upon the heart of the believer, is Allah Most High Himself. Allah gives Himself the Name of 'Faithful' in His Qur'ān:

> *He is Allah besides whom there is no god. . . The Faithful,* [Guardian of the Faith], *the Guardian overall.* (Sūra Ḥashr, 23)

The home of the sultan-soul in the hereafter is *Firdaws*—the heavenly paradise.

The station where the holy spirit reigns is the secret place that Allah made for Himself in the centre of the heart where He deposited His Secret (*sirr*) for safekeeping. The state of this soul is described by Allah speaking through His Prophet ﷺ: 'Man is My secret and I am the secret of man.' Its business is the truth which is obtained by achieving unity; that is its work. It brings multiplicity into unity by continuously reciting the names of unity in the language of the divine secret. This is not an audible exterior language.

> *And if you utter the saying aloud, surely He knows the secret and what is yet more hidden.* (Sūra Ṭā Hā, 7)

Only Allah hears the language of the holy spirit, only Allah knows its state.

The benefit of this soul is the vision of the first-created creation. What it sees is Allah's beauty. To it belongs the secret vision. Seeing and hearing become one. There is no comparison, there is no resemblance to anything in what it sees. It sees Allah's attributes of might and wrath as one with His attributes of beauty, grace and mercy.

When man finds his goal, his home, as he finds the causal intelligence, his worldly mind that led him until then comes under its command: his heart is in awe, his tongue is tied. He has no power to give the news of these states because Allah is exempt from any resemblance to anything conceivable.

When what is said here reaches the ears of the ones who know, let them first try to understand the level of their knowledge. Let them bring all their attention to the true reality of the things they know before they raise their eyes to the further horizons, before they seek to reach new heights, that they may reach the level of the knowledge of divine providence. May they not deny what has been said, but seek the wisdom to find unity, oneness. That is essential.

CHAPTER FOUR

On Knowledge

OUTER knowledge of things that are self-evident is divided into twelve sections, and inner knowledge is also in twelve sections. These portions are divided among the common people and the special, pure servants of Allah in proportion to their potential.

For our purposes these sciences are in four sections. The first concerns the precepts of the religion regarding obligations and interdictions related to things and actions of this world. The second concerns the inner meaning and reason for these precepts, and is called the science of the conceptual knowledge of things that are not self-evident, the mystical sciences. The third concerns the hidden spiritual essence itself, which is called wisdom. The fourth concerns the inner essence of this essence, which is the truth. The perfect man must learn and know all of these and find paths leading to them.

Our Master the Prophet ﷺ said, 'The religion is a tree: mysticism is its branches, wisdom is its foliage, truth is its fruit. The Holy Qur'ān, with its commentaries, explanations, interpretations and analogies, contains them all.' In the book *al-Majma*ʿ the words *tafsīr*, 'commentary', and *ta'wīl*, 'interpretation through analogies', are defined thus: 'Commentary on the Qur'ān is clarification and elaboration for the understanding of the common people, while interpretation through analogy is clarification of the inner meaning through inspired reflections experienced by the true believer. Such interpretation is for those special servants of Allah who are firmly established, constant in their spiritual state and well-grounded in the knowledge that enables them to form true judgments. Like the date-tree whose roots are firm in the ground, their feet are firm in this material world; and again like the date-tree, whose fronds reach high into the sky, their hearts and minds are raised to heavenly knowledge.' By the grace of Allah this constancy that contains no doubts is placed in the centre of their hearts. The heart firm in this state is likened to the second half of the Confession of Unity *Lā ilāha illā Llāh*, 'There is no god but Allah'—*illā Llāh*, 'only Allah', is the final confirmation of unity.

> *He it is Who has revealed the Book to thee; some of its verses are decisive—they are the basis of the Book—and others are allegorical. Then those in whose hearts is perversity follow the part of it which is allegorical, seeking to mislead, and seeking to give it* (their own) *interpretation. And none knows its interpretation save Allah and those firmly rooted in knowledge* (al-rāsikhūn). *They say: We believe in it, it is all from our Lord. And none are mindful except men of understanding.* (Sūra Āl ʿImrān, 7)

The writer of a great commentary on the Qur'ān says about this verse, 'If the door in this verse would open, all the doors of the inner secret realm would open too'.

The true servant of Allah is obliged to fulfill Allah's orders and to abstain from what He forbids. He is also obliged to oppose his ego and the lower dictates of his flesh. The basic opposition of the ego to religion is in the form of imagination and illusions contrary to reality. On the level of mysticism, the treacherous ego encourages one to agree with and to follow causes and propositions that are only close to truth, even to follow prophetic messages and declarations of saints that have been distorted and to follow false teachers and ideas. On the level of wisdom, the ego tries to push one to claim sainthood, even divinity—the worst sin of setting oneself up as a partner to Allah. Allah says: *Seest thou such a one as taketh for his god his own passion* (or impulse)... (Sūra Furqān, 43).

But the level of truth is different. Neither the ego nor the Devil can reach there—not even the angels set foot there. Anyone but Allah who approached there would burn to ashes, as the angel Gabriel عليه السلام said to the Prophet ﷺ at the edge of that level, when he declared, 'If I take another step, I will burn to ashes'.

The true servant of Allah is free from the opposition of his ego and the Devil, because he is protected by a shield of sincerity and purity.

> *He* [the accursed Devil] *said: Then by Thy Might! I will surely lead them astray, except Thy servants from among them who are sincere and pure.* (Sūra Ṣād, 82–83)

Man cannot attain the truth unless he is pure, because his worldly attributes will not leave him until the essence is manifested in him. This is true sincerity. His ignorance will only leave him when he receives the knowledge of Allah's Essence. One cannot obtain this with education; only Allah, without intermediaries, can teach it. When Allah Most High is Himself the teacher, He gives one knowledge from Himself, as He did for the prophet Khiḍr. Then man, with the consciousness of what he has received, reaches the level of divine wisdom, where he knows his Lord and worships Him Whom he knows.

One who reaches this state has the vision of the holy spirit and comes to see the Beloved of Allah, Muḥammad ﷺ. He talks with him about all and everything from the beginning to the end, and all the other prophets give him the good tidings of the promise of union with the Beloved. Allah describes this state:

> *And whoever obeys Allah and the Messenger, they are with those upon whom Allah has bestowed favours from among the prophets and the truthful and the faithful and the righteous, and a goodly company are they!* (Sūra Nisā', 69)

One who cannot find this knowledge in his being will not become wise even if he reads a million books. The benefit for which one may hope in acquiring the outer knowledge of self-evident things is perhaps Paradise: there all that will be seen is the manifestation of divine attributes in shapes of light. No matter how perfect his knowledge of the visible and conceivable may be, it will not help man to enter into the sanctity of the sacred place, the place close to Allah, for one has to fly to that place and to fly one needs two wings. The true servant of Allah is the one who flies to that realm with the wings of the outer and the inner knowledge, never stopping on the way, never being distracted by anything in his flight. Allah, speaking through His Prophet ﷺ, says:

> My servant, if you wish to enter the sanctuary of My intimacy, do not pay attention either to this world or to the higher world of the angels, not even to the higher realms where you may receive My divine attributes.

This material world is the temptation, the devil, of the man of knowledge. The angelic realm is the temptation of the wise, and the realm of the divine attributes is the temptation of the one who is cognizant of the truth. Whoever is satisfied with one of them is rejected from Allah's grace of bringing him close to His Essence. If they give in to these temptations, they stop, they do not advance, they soar no higher. Though their goal was to be close to their Creator, they cannot reach there any longer. They become distracted; they are the ones with a single wing.

The one who becomes aware of truth receives such grace, such gifts from Allah that no worldly eye has seen the like, nor any worldly ear heard it, nor worldly heart known its names. This is the paradise of intimacy. There are neither palaces of jewels, nor ever-beautiful maidens as companions there. May man know his own worth and not want nor claim that which is not his due! Ḥaḍrat 'Alī, may Allah be pleased with him, says: 'May Allah shower His Beneficence upon the one who knows his worth, who knows to stay within his bounds, who watches his tongue, who does not spend this life in idleness.'

The man who knows must be aware that the child of the spirit which is born in his heart is the meaning of true humanity: that is the true human being. He should educate the child of the heart, teaching unity through constantly being aware of unity—leaving this world of matter and of multiplicity, seeking the spiritual world, the world of mysteries, where there is none other than the Essence of Allah. In reality there is no other place but that place, which has no end, no beginning. The child of the heart soars over that infinite field seeing things that none have seen before, none could tell of, none could describe. That place is the home of those who left themselves behind and found unity with their Lord, who saw what they saw with the same eye as their Lord, the eye of unity When they see the beauty and the grace of their Lord there is nothing of their temporal being left in them. If one looks at the sun one can see nothing else, neither can one see oneself. When Allah's beauty and grace are manifest, what could be left of oneself? Nothing.

Jesus عليه السلام said, 'Man has to be born twice to reach the realm of the angels, like the birds who are born twice.' It is the birth of the meaning from the act, the birth of the spirit from the flesh. That possibility is in man. That is the mystery, the secret of man. It is born of the intercourse of man's knowledge of the religion and man's awareness of the truth, as all children are born of the union of two drops of water.

> *Verily We created man from a drop of seminal fluid, in order to try him. So We gave him* (the gifts) *of hearing and sight.* (Sūra Insān, 2)

When meaning becomes manifest in being, it becomes easy to pass through the shallows into the sea of creation and to immerse oneself in the depth of Allah's commandments. All of the material universes are but a drop in comparison to the sea of the spiritual world. It is only when all this is understood that the spiritual power and light of the mysteries of divine nature, the real truth, emanate into the world without words and without sound.

CHAPTER FIVE

On Repentance and On Teaching by the Word

CERTAIN levels and stages in man's spiritual evolution have been mentioned: let it be known that each of these levels is obtained primarily through repentance. The way to repent can only be learned from someone who knows how to repent and who has himself repented. True and total repentance is the first step.

> *When those who disbelieved harboured disdain in their hearts, the disdain of ignorance, Allah sent down His tranquillity on His Messenger and on the believers and made them keep the word of the fear of Allah* (repentance). *And then they were entitled to and worthy of it, and Allah is full knower of all things.* (Sūra Fatḥ, 26)

The state of the fear of Allah has the same meaning as *Lā ilāha illā Llāh*: there is no god, there is nothing—but Allah. For the one who knows this has the fear of losing Him, losing His beneficence, His love, His mercy; he fears and is ashamed to do wrong under His very eye and fears His punishment. If one is not oneself such a person, one must find someone who is and receive this fear of Allah from him.

The source from which this word is received has to be purified and cleansed of everything other than Allah, and whoever receives it should have the ability to differentiate between the words of one with a purified heart and those pronounced by the tongue of the common man. The receiver should also be aware of the way in which the word is pronounced, for words that sound the same may mean totally different things. It is impossible that the word coming from a pure source be the same as the word coming from elsewhere.

The heart is enlivened only when it receives the seed of unity from a living heart, because such a seed is a healthy, living seed. Nothing grows from a seed that is dry and lifeless. The sacred word *Lā ilāha illā Llāh* mentioned in two places in the Holy Qur'ān is a proof:

> *They indeed were arrogant when it was said to them, 'There is no god but Allah', and they said, 'Shall we give up our gods?'* (Sūra Ṣāffāt, 35–36)

This is the state of the common man, for whom outer appearances, including his own outer existence, are gods.

> *So know that there is no god but Allah, and ask forgiveness for your sin and for the believing man and believing woman, for Allah knows what you do wherever you go and how you live in* [the secrecy of] *your houses.* (Sūra Muḥammad, 19)

These words of Allah are the guide for those pure believers who fear Allah.

Ḥaḍrat 'Alī, may Allah be pleased with him, asked our Master the Prophet ﷺ to teach him the easiest, the most valuable, the most immediate way to his salvation. Our Master the Prophet ﷺ waited for the angel Gabriel عليه السلام to bring the answer from the Divine Source. He came and taught our Master to say *Lā ilāha*— 'There is no god' while turning his blessed face to the right, and to say *illā Llāh*—'but Allah alone' while turning his face to the left, towards his blessed pure heart. He repeated this three times; our Master ﷺ himself repeated it three times and then taught it to Ḥaḍrat 'Alī, may Allah be pleased with him, making him repeat it three times. Then he taught the divine Confession of Unity in the same manner to his Companions. Ḥaḍrat 'Alī was the first to ask for it and was the first to be taught.

Then one day, when they had just returned from a great battle, the Prophet ﷺ said to his followers, 'We have returned from a small battle to wage the great war,' indicating the struggle with one's own ego, one's lower self, which is the meaning of the Confession of Unity. 'Your greatest enemy', he said, 'is under your ribs'.

The divine love will not come alive in you until the enemy, the desires of your flesh, dies and leaves you.

First you must be cleansed of that ego that commands your whole being to evil: then you will have a partial conscience, although continuing to sin. You will have a feeling of self-reproach—but this is not enough. You must pass beyond that stage to the level where the truth will be revealed to you, the truth of the right and the wrong. Then you will stop doing wrong and do that which is right; thus your being will be cleansed. Opposing your flesh, you must fight against its animal desires—gluttony, excessive sleep, idle occupations—and against the characteristics of the wild beast in you: negativity, anger, fighting, aggressiveness. Then you must work to rid yourself of the evil habits of the ego: arrogance, pride, envy, vengeance, greed and all the other afflictions and sicknesses of the body and of the heart. Only those who are able to do these things are truly repentant and are cleansed and pure.

> *For Allah loves those who turn to Him constantly* (in repentance), *and He loves those who keep themselves pure and clean.* (Sūra Baqara, 222)

In one's repentance one must be heedful that one's regret is not abstract and general, so that it does not fall under the threat of Allah's declaration, *No matter how much they repent, they are not truly penitent*, and *Their repentance is not accepted.* This refers to those who have merely pronounced the words of regret, but neither know the extent of their sin, nor have vowed not to sin again, nor have taken any action. That is ordinary repentance, the outer repentance, which does not penetrate to the cause of the sin. It is as if such people are trying to get rid of grass by cutting it off at the ground rather than digging out its roots. In doing this, they only help it to grow better. The one who repents knowing his fault and the cause of his fault and wishing to rid himself of this fault, digs out the roots of this pernicious plant. When it is dug out, it dries, and it does not come back again. The trowel used in digging the roots, the causes of one's sins, is the spiritual teaching one receives from a true teacher. One must clear the ground before one can plant one's orchard.

And We set forth the parables to man that he may reflect. (Sūra Ḥashr, 21)

He is the one who accepts repentance from His servants and forgives sins, and He knows all that you do. (Sūra Shūrā, 25)

And whoever repents and believes and works righteous deeds, Allah changes his evil deeds into good ones, and Allah is Ever-Forgiving, Merciful. (Sūra Furqān, 70)

Know that the sign that repentance is accepted is that the sin never occurs in one again.

There are two kinds of repentance, the repentance of the common man and the repentance of the pure believer. The common man hopes to pass from evil deeds to righteousness through remembering Allah and exercising serious effort, leaving the desires and comfort of his flesh and forcing difficulties upon his ego. He must pass from egotistical revolt against Allah's precepts to obedience. That is his repentance, which may bring him from hellfire into Paradise.

The pure believers, the true servants of Allah, are in altogether a different state. They are at the level of divine wisdom, which is far higher than the best state of the ordinary man. In fact, for them there are no longer steps to climb: they have reached the proximity of Allah. They have left the pleasures and benefits of this world and are tasting the delightful flavour of the spiritual realm—the taste of the intimacy of Allah, the pleasure of seeing His Essence with the eye of certitude.

The perception of common men is the common world, and their pleasure is in tasting the material benefits of material existence. Yet while the very existence of the material man and the material world is an error, so too are the best benefits and pleasures of it. As the great saying goes, 'Your existence is such a sin that all other sins are small in comparison with it.' The wise have often claimed that many good deeds done by good men who have not reached the level of Allah's intimacy are no better than the errors of those who have come close to Allah. Thus in order to teach us to ask forgiveness for the hidden errors that we think of as good deeds, our Prophet ﷺ, who was sinless, used to seek forgiveness one hundred times a day. Allah Most High asked him to *ask forgiveness for your sins and for the believing men and believing women* (Sūra Muḥammad, 19). He set the pure Prophet as an example of how to repent—by begging Allah to erase one's ego, one's personality, one's individuality, all of oneself, to take away one's very existence. This is true repentance.

Penitence means to renounce everything with the exception of Allah's Essence, and to wish to return to Him, to return to the home of His intimacy, to see the Divine Face. Our Master, the Beloved of Allah, described such penitents, saying, 'There are some true servants of Allah whose bodies are here but whose hearts are up under the Throne of Allah.' Their hearts are in the ninth heaven, under the Throne of Allah, because the divine vision of His Essence is impossible in the world below.

Here only the manifestation of His divine attributes can be viewed, reflected upon the pure mirrors of pure hearts: as Ḥaḍrat 'Umar (may God be pleased with him) said, 'My heart saw my Lord with the light of my Lord'. The pure heart is a mirror where the beauty, grace, and perfection of Allah is reflected. Another name given to this state is 'revelation', beholding the divine attributes.

To reach that state, to clean and shine that heart, one needs a teacher who is mature, who is in union with Allah, and who is esteemed by all, past and present. That teacher has to have reached a stage close to Allah and to have been sent back to this lower realm by Allah to perfect those who are worthy, but lacking.

In their coming down for this task such saintly men of Allah must travel the way of the Prophet ﷺ and follow his example, yet their function is distinct from the function of the Prophet. While prophets are sent for the salvation of common people as well as pure believers, these teachers are not sent to teach everybody, but only a select number. While prophets are given total independence in carrying out their duties, these saintly teachers are not independent, but must follow the way and example of the Prophet.

It is said that a spiritual teacher who declares himself independent wishes to liken himself to a prophet, which will lead him to blasphemy and infidelity. When our Prophet ﷺ stated that his wise companions are like the prophets of the Israelites, his meaning was other than this—for the prophets who came after Moses عليه السلام all followed the religious principles that Moses عليه السلام brought. They did not bring new precepts. They followed the same laws. Like them, the wise among the people of Muḥammad ﷺ , whose function is to teach the select few among the pure, follow the wisdom of the Prophet ﷺ, yet present the ordinances and that which is forbidden in a different and new way, open and clear, showing their students good deeds with the example of their own righteous acts performed at a different time and in different circumstances. They encourage their followers by pointing out the joy and beauty of the principles of the religion. Their aim is to help their followers to clear their hearts, which are sites for building the monument of wisdom.

In all this they follow the example of those disciples of the Prophet ﷺ who were called 'the people of the woollen garb', who had abandoned all worldly activity to stand at the gate of the Prophet ﷺ and be close to him. Those disciples gave news as they received it, directly from the mouth of the Prophet ﷺ. In their closeness to the Prophet ﷺ they reached such a level that they were able to talk about the mysteries of the ascension of the Prophet ﷺ even before he revealed these secrets to his Companions.

These saintly teachers possess a closeness similar to that of the Prophet ﷺ to his Lord: a similar trust and guardianship of divine knowledge is bestowed upon them. They are the bearers of a part of prophethood, and their inner being is secure under the guardianship of the Prophet ﷺ himself.

Not everyone who possesses knowledge is in such a state. The ones who have reached it are closer to the Prophet ﷺ than to their own sons and family and are like his spiritual sons with an affinity closer than mere blood relationship. They are the true inheritors of the Prophet ﷺ. A true son possesses his father's essence and secret both in his exterior appearance and in his inner being. The Prophet ﷺ explains this secret as '. . . a special knowledge like a hidden treasure that only those who know the Essence of Allah can find. Yet when the mystery is revealed, no one who is conscious and sincere can deny it.'

That knowledge was placed in our Master ﷺ during the Night Voyage, his ascension to his Lord. That mystery was hidden in him behind thirty thousand veils. He did not reveal its secret except to those among his disciples who were closest to him. It is by the propagation and blessing of this secret that Islam will continue to reign until the last day of the worlds.

It is the inner knowledge of what is hidden that leads one to that secret. The worldly sciences, arts and skills are as the shell of that inner knowledge, yet the ones who are skilled in these may hope one day to possess what is in that shell. Some of these men of knowledge possess only what it is obligatory for a human being to possess and others become masters and preserve knowledge from being lost. Yet others call humanity to Allah with good advice. Some of them follow the way of Muḥammad ﷺ and are led to Ḥaḍrat 'Alī, who is the gate to knowledge through which enter those who are invited by divine invitation.

> *Invite to the way of thy Lord with wisdom and good preaching and argue with them in ways that are best and most gracious.* (Sūra Naḥl, 125)

What they mean in their words is the same. Its appearance of difference is only a matter of details and manner of expression.

Actually, there are three meanings that appear as three different kinds of knowledge—acted upon differently, but converging into one in the tradition of our Master the Prophet ﷺ. Knowledge is divided into three, for no single person can carry that whole load of knowledge, nor is able to act upon it.

The first part of the verse, *Invite to the way of thy Lord with wisdom*, corresponds to the divine wisdom, the essence and beginning of all and everything. Its possessor must, like the Prophet ﷺ, act in accordance with it. It is only given to the true and brave man, the spiritual warrior who will defend his position and fight to preserve that knowledge. Our Master describes him thus: 'The zealous effort of the true man can shake the mountains'—the 'mountain' meaning the heaviness of the hearts of some. The prayers of these men are accepted. When they wish for something, it happens; when they wish something to disappear, it evaporates.

> *He grants wisdom to whom He pleases, and he to whom wisdom is granted receives indeed a benefit overflowing.*
> (Sūra Baqara, 269)

The second is the outer knowledge indicated in the Qur'ānic verse as 'good preaching'. It is the shell of inner wisdom. The ones who possess it preach the good and teach good action and forbid man what Allah has forbidden. The Prophet ﷺ praises them. The man of knowledge preaches with kindness and gentleness, while the ignorant man teaches with harshness and anger.

The third knowledge is concerned with regulating worldly human affairs. It is the husk over religious knowledge, which is the shell over divine wisdom. It is the knowledge destined for those who rule men: man's justice over man, man's government of man. The last part of the Qur'ānic verse previously mentioned describes their function: *and argue with them in ways that are best and most gracious*. Such people are the manifestation of Allah's attribute of *al-Qahhār,* the Overpowering Dominator. Their function is the maintenance of order among men in accordance with Divine Law, as the husk protects the shell—while the outer knowledge, which is the shell, protects the inner knowledge, which is the seed.

The Prophet ﷺ advises, 'Frequent the company of wise men, obey your just rulers. Allah Most High revives dead hearts with wisdom as He makes the dead earth come alive with vegetation by means of His rain.' He also says, 'Wisdom is the lost property of the believer. He picks it up wherever he finds it.'

Even the words pronounced by ordinary men have descended from the Preserved Tablet of Allah's decrees concerning all things happening from the beginning until the end. That Tablet is kept in the high realm of causal intelligence, yet words are pronounced in accordance with one's level. The words of those who have reached the level of truth are directly from that realm, the realm of Allah's intimacy. There is no intermediary there.

Know that all will return to its origin. The heart, the essence, has to be awakened, made alive, to find its way back to its divine origin. It has to hear the call. One has to find the one through whom the call will come, the true teacher. That is an obligation upon one. The Prophet says. 'Knowledge is an obligation upon every Muslim, woman and man.' That knowledge is the final stage of all knowledge, the divine wisdom, the knowledge which will lead one to one's origin, to the truth. The rest of knowledge is necessary only to the extent that it is useful. Yet for the sake of one's ego, one is ambitious for worldly knowledge. Allah is pleased with those who leave ambition for worldly honours and fame, for these worldly benefits are what hinder one in one's voyage to Him.

> *Say: I ask of you nothing in return for this but love and attachment to those near of kin.* (Sūra Shūrā, 23)

According to tradition, the meaning of the words 'what is close to you' is to come close to truth.

CHAPTER SIX

On Islamic Mysticism and the Sufis

THE name *ṣufī* is an expression derived from the Arabic word *ṣāf*, 'pure'. The reason that the Sufis are called by this name is that their inner world is purified and enlightened with the light of wisdom, unity and oneness.

Another meaning for this appellation is that they are spiritually connected with the constant companions of the Prophet who were called 'the companions with the woollen garb'.

They may also have worn the customary garb of rough-woven sheep's wool (*ṣūf*) when they were novices, and have spent their life in old patched clothes.

As their exterior is poor and humble, so is their worldly life. They are frugal in eating, drinking and other pleasures of this world. In the book called *al-Majma*ʿ it is said, 'What is becoming to the pious ascetic is the most ordinary and humble clothing and way of living.' Although they may appear unattractive to the worldly, their wisdom is manifested in their gentleness and delicate manner, which make them attractive to those who know. In reality they are an example to mankind. They follow divine prescriptions. They are, in the sight of their Lord, in the first rank of humanity; in the eyes of those who seek their Lord they are beautiful despite their humble appearance. They must be distinguished and distinguishable and they must be that way one and all, for they are all on the level of unity and oneness and must appear as one.

In Arabic the word *taṣawwuf*, Islamic mysticism, consists of four consonants, *t, ṣ, w* and *f*. The first letter, *t*, stands for *tawba*, repentance. This is the first step to be taken on the path. It is as if it were a double step, one outward and one inward. The outward step in repentance is in words and deeds and feelings: to keep one's life free from sin and from wrongdoing and to incline towards obedience; to flee from revolt and opposition, to seek agreement and harmony. The inner step of repentance is taken by the heart. It is the cleansing of the heart from conflicting worldly desires and the heart's total affirmation of the wish for the divine. Repentance—to be aware of the wrong and to abandon it, to be conscious of the right and to strive for it—brings one to the second step.

The second stage is the state of peace and joy, *ṣafā'*. The letter *ṣ* is its symbol. In this stage there are similarly two steps to take: the first is towards purity in heart and the second towards its secret centre.

Peace of heart comes of a heart free of anxiety. Anxiety is caused by the weight of all that is material—the weight of food, of drink, of sleep, of idle talk. All this, like the gravity of the earth, pulls the ethereal heart downwards, and to free itself from this weight tires the heart. Then there are ties—desire, possessions, love of family and children—which bind the ethereal heart to the earth and keep it from soaring.

The way to free the heart, to purify it, is to remember Allah. At the beginning this remembrance can only be done outwardly, by repeating His divine Names, pronouncing them aloud so that you yourself and others can hear and remember. As the memory of Him becomes constant, remembrance sinks to the heart and becomes inward, silent. Allah says:

> *Believers are those who, when Allah is mentioned, feel a tremor in their hearts, and when they* [see and] *hear His manifestations their faith is strengthened.* (Sūra Anfāl, 2)

'Tremor' means the awe, fear, and love of Allah. With this remembrance and recitation of Allah's Names the heart wakes up from the sleep of heedlessness, is cleansed, is shined. Then forms and shapes from the hidden unseen realm are reflected in that heart. The Prophet ﷺ says, 'The men of knowledge outwardly visit and inspect things with their minds, while the wise are inwardly busy cleaning and shining their hearts.'

The peace of the secret centre of the heart is achieved by cleansing the heart of each and every thing and preparing it to receive Allah's Essence alone, which enters the heart when that heart is beautified with the love of the divine. The means of this cleansing is the constant inward remembrance and recital with the secret tongue of the divine Confession of Unity *lā ilāha illā Llāh*—'there is no god but Allah'. When the heart and its centre are in a state of peace and joy, then the second stage, represented by the letter *ṣ*, is complete.

The third letter, *w*, stands for *wilāya*, which is the state of sanctity of the lovers and friends of Allah. This state depends upon inner purity. Allah mentions His friends in the Holy Qur'ān:

> *Be heedful; verily upon the friends of Allah there is no fear, nor do they grieve.*
>
> *For them there are glad tidings in this life and in the hereafter. . .* (Sūra Yūnus, 62 and 64)

The one in this state of sanctity is totally conscious of, in love with and connected to Allah. As a result he is beautified with the best of character, morals and manners. This is a divine gift bestowed upon him. Our Master the Prophet ﷺ said, 'Observe divine morals and behave in accordance with them'. At that stage the conscious man sheds his worldly, temporal characteristics and appears clad in divine attributes. Allah says through His Prophet ﷺ:

> When I love My servant I become his eyes, his ears, his tongue, his hands and his feet. He sees through Me, he hears through Me, he speaks in My name, his hands become Mine and he walks with Me.

Cleanse yourself of everything and keep only Allah's Essence in you, for:

> *the Truth has come and falsehood vanished. Surely falsehood is ever bound to vanish.* (Sūra Banī Isrā'īl, 81)

When the truth comes and falsehood has vanished, the level of *wilāya* is complete.

The fourth letter, *f* stands for *fanā'* the annihilation of self, the state of nothingness. The false self melts and evaporates when divine attributes enter one's being, and when the multiplicity of worldly attributes and personalities leave, their place is taken by the single attribute of unity.

In reality, the truth is always present. It neither disappears nor declines. What happens is that the believer realizes and becomes one with that which has created him. In being with Him, the believer receives His pleasure: the temporal being finds its true existence by realizing the eternal secret. *Everything will perish but His Countenance...* (Sūra Qaṣaṣ, 88)

The way to realize His truth is through His pleasure, through His agreement. When you do deeds for His sake which meet with His approval you come close to His truth, His Essence. Then all disappears except the One Who is pleased and the one with whom He is pleased, united. Good deeds are the mother that bears the child of truth: the conscious life of a true human being. *The good words and the good deeds rise to Allah.* (Sūra Fāṭir, 10). If one acts and exists for anything but Allah's sake alone, one is setting up partners to Allah, putting oneself or others in the place of Allah—the unforgivable sin that sooner or later destroys one. But when the self and selfishness are annihilated, one reaches the stage of union with Allah. The level of union is in the realm of Allah's proximity. Allah describes this realm thus:

> *Surely the righteous will be... in the place of truth, in the presence of a Sovereign Omnipotent.*
> (Sūra Qamar, 54–55)

That place is the place of the essential truth, the truth of all truths, the place of unity and oneness. It is the place reserved for prophets, for the ones who are loved by Allah, for His friends. Allah is with those who are true. When a created existence is united with the eternal existence, it cannot be conceived as a separate existence. When all earthly ties are abandoned and one is in union with Allah, with the divine truth, one receives eternal purity, never to be blemished, and becomes one of the *companions of the garden, therein to dwell* (forever). (Sūra Aʿrāf, 42). They are: *Those who believe and work righteousness*, (Sūra Aʿrāf, 42). However, *no burden do We place on any soul, but that which it can bear.* (Sūra Aʿrāf, 42) But one needs a great deal of patience. *And Allah is with those who patiently persevere.* (Sūra Anfāl, 66)

CHAPTER SEVEN

On Remembrance

ALLAH Most High Himself shows the way to those who seek to remember Him. *Remember Allah as He has guided you...* (Sūra Baqara, 198). This means to remember that your Creator has brought you to a certain level of consciousness and faith and that you can only remember Him in accordance with this ability. Our Master the Prophet ﷺ says, 'The best declaration of remembrance is the one which I and all the prophets before me recite. It is in the divine phrase *Lā ilāha illā Llāh*—"there is no god but Allah".'

There are different levels of remembrance and each has different ways. Some are expressed outwardly with audible voice, some felt inwardly, silently, from the centre of the heart. At the beginning one should declare in words what one remembers. Then stage by stage the remembrance spreads throughout one's being—descending to the heart, then rising to the soul; then still further it reaches the realm of the secrets; further to the hidden; to the most hidden of the hidden. How far the remembrance penetrates, the level it reaches, depends solely on the extent to which Allah in His bounty has guided one.

Remembrance pronounced in words is but a declaration that the heart has not forgotten Allah. The inward silent remembrance is a movement of the emotions. The remembrance of the heart is through feeling in oneself the manifestation of Allah's might and beauty, while the remembrance of the soul is through the enlightenment of the divine light generated by Allah's might and beauty. The remembrance of the level of the secret realm is through the ecstasy received from beholding the divine secrets. The remembrance of the hidden realm brings one to: *the place of truth in the presence of a Sovereign Omnipotent.* (Sūra Qamar, 55) The remembrance at the final level that is called *khafī al-akhfā'*—'the most hidden of the hidden'—brings one to a state of annihilation of the self and unification with the truth. In reality none other than Allah knows the state of the one who has penetrated into that realm containing all knowledge, which is the end of all and everything. *Surely He knows the secret and what is yet more hidden.* (Sūra Ṭā Hā, 7)

When one has passed through these stages of remembrance, a different state of spirit, as if a different soul, is born in one. That soul is purer and finer than all other souls. It is the child of the heart, the child of truth. While in the form of seed, this child invites and attracts man to seek and find the truth; and after it is born this child will urge man to seek the Essence of Allah Most High. Neither this new soul called the child of the heart, nor its seed and potential, is in every man. It is found only in the pure believer: *He places the soul with His decree in the hearts of those whom He chooses.* (Sūra Mu'min, 15)

This soul is sent from the realm of the All-powerful and is placed in the universe of the visible worlds where the attributes of the Creator are manifest in the creation, but it belongs to the realm of truth. It does not favour nor pay any attention to anything but the Essence of Allah. Our Master the Prophet ﷺ explains: 'This world is undesirable and unlawful for those who wish for the hereafter. The hereafter is undesirable for those who wish for this world, and it will not be given to them. But for the souls who seek Allah's Essence, neither this world nor the hereafter has any attraction.' This soul is the child of truth. It is that within one which will seek, find and be with its Lord.

Over and above anything you do, the material being in you must follow the straight path. That is only possible through preserving and following the precepts of religion. To do this one has to be conscious, to remember—to remember Allah, night and day, inwardly and outwardly, continuously. For those who see the truth, to remember Allah is an obligation. As Allah orders:

> *Remember Allah standing and sitting and lying down.* (Sūra Nisā', 103)

> . . . *those who remember Allah standing and sitting and lying on their sides, and who reflect on the creation of the heavens and the earth. Our Lord, Thou hast not created this in vain! Glory be to thee. . .* (Sūra Āl 'Imrān, 191)

CHAPTER EIGHT

The Necessary Conditions for Remembrance

ONE of the conditions that prepares one to remember is to be in a state of ablution; washed and cleansed bodily and purified inwardly. At the beginning, a condition for the effectiveness of remembrance is to pronounce aloud the words and phrases of what is to be remembered—the Confession of Unity, the attributes of Allah. When these words are recited, one should use all one's effort to be in a conscious state. In this way the heart hears the word and is enlightened with the light of that which is remembered. It receives energy and becomes alive — not only alive in this world, but alive forever in the hereafter. Allah Most High describes this eternal life: *They taste not therein death, except the first death...* (Sūra Dukhān, 56)

Our Master the Prophet ﷺ describing the state of the believer who achieves truth through remembrance, says, 'Believers do not die. They only pass from this temporal life to the everlasting life'. And they do there what they did here. As he says, 'The prophets and the ones close to Allah continue their worship in their graves as they did in their houses.' The worship he mentions is inward supplication of Allah, not the prayer obligatory five times a day in this world, with its standing, bowing and prostration. Inward silent supplication is one of the principal qualities identifying the true believer.

Wisdom is not obtained by man, but is given to him by Allah. After having been elevated to that state, the wise become intimate with the secrets of Allah. Allah brings one to His secrets only if one's heart is alive and conscious with the remembrance of Him, and if that conscious heart has the wish to receive the truth. As our Master the Prophet ﷺ says, 'My eyes sleep, but my heart is ever awake'.

The importance of wishing in obtaining wisdom and truth is explained in the words of our Prophet ﷺ, 'If a person wishes to learn and acts upon his wish and studies, but dies before attaining his goal, Allah assigns him two angels as teachers who teach him divine wisdom until the Day of Judgment. That person is raised from his grave as a wise man who has obtained the truth.' The two angels here represent the spirit of our Prophet and the light of love and sanctity which connects man with Allah. The importance of wish and intention is further mentioned by the Prophet ﷺ: 'Many who wish to know die ignorant, but they are raised from their graves on the Day of Judgment as wise; and many a man of knowledge is raised on that day depraved, having lost everything, and totally ignorant.' Those men who are proud of their knowledge, who seek knowledge in order to obtain the goods of the world and to sin, are warned:

> *You received your good things in the life of the world and you took your pleasure from them, but today shall you be recompensed with a penalty of humiliation, for that you were arrogant on earth without just cause and that you* (even) *transgressed.* (Sūra Aḥqāf, 20)

The Prophet ﷺ says, 'Actions are conditioned by and tied to intentions. The wish and intention of the faithful are better and more worthy in the sight of Allah than are his actions. The intention of the unfaithful is worse than what appears in his actions. For Allah, the good intention of the believer is more worthy than the best deed of the unfaithful.' Intention is the foundation of action. Our Master the Prophet ﷺ says, 'It is good to build a good deed upon a good foundation, and a sin is a deed built upon bad intentions.'

> *Whoso desires the cultivation of the hereafter We give him increase in his cultivation, and whoso desires the cultivation of this world We give him thereof and he has no portion in the hereafter.* (Sūra Shūrā, 20)

The best course is to find a true spiritual teacher who will bring your heart to life. This will secure you the eternal life of the hereafter. This is urgent; it has to be done immediately in this life before the time is spent. This world is the field of the hereafter. He who does not plant here will not reap there. So plant your field upon this earth with both the subjective seeds of a good life here and the objective seeds that will yield a good harvest in the hereafter.

CHAPTER NINE

On the Vision of Allah: Arriving at the Level of Seeing the Manifestation of the Divine Essence

THE VISION of Allah is of two kinds: one is seeing the manifestation of Allah's attribute of Perfect Beauty directly in the hereafter, and the other is seeing the manifestation of the divine attributes reflected upon the clear mirror of the pure heart, in this life, in this world. In such a case the vision appears as the manifestation of light emanating from the Perfect Beauty of Allah and is seen by the eye of the essence of the heart.

Allah describes the vision seen by the eye of the heart: *The heart did not deny what it saw.* (Sūra Najm, 11)

On seeing the manifestation of the divine through an intermediary the Prophet ﷺ says, 'The faithful is the mirror of the faithful'. What is meant by the first 'faithful', the mirror in this phrase, is the pure heart of the believer, while the second 'faithful' Who sees His reflection in that mirror is Allah Most High. Whoever arrives at the level of seeing the manifestations of Allah's attributes in the world will certainly see the Essence of Allah in the hereafter without shape or form.

The reality of this has been confirmed by many of the beloved and the lovers of Allah. Ḥaḍrat 'Umar, may Allah be pleased with him, said, 'My heart saw my Lord by the Light of my Lord'. And Ḥaḍrat 'Alī, may Allah be pleased with him, said, 'I will not pray to

Allah unless I see Him'. They both must have seen the manifestation of divine attributes. If someone sees sunlight coming through the windows and says, 'I see the sun!' he is telling the truth.

Allah gives the most beautiful example of the manifestation of His attributes.

> *Allah is the Light of the heavens and the earth. The parable of His light is as if there were a niche and within it a lamp, the lamp enclosed in glass, the glass as it were a brilliant star lit from a blessed tree, an olive neither of the East nor of the West, whose oil is well-nigh luminous, though fire scarce touches it; light upon light! Allah doth guide whom He will to His light.* (Sūra Nūr, 35)

The meaning of the niche is the faithful heart of the believer. The lamp enlightening the niche of the heart is the essence of the heart, while the light that it sheds is the divine secret, the sultan-soul. The glass is transparent and does not keep the light within, but protects it and allows it to spread, which is why it is likened to a star. The source of the light is a divine tree. That tree is the state of unity reaching out with its branches and its roots, inculcating the principles of faith, communicating without any intermediary in the language of purity.

It is directly in this language of purity that our Master the Prophet ﷺ received the Qur'ānic revelations. In reality, the angel Gabriel brought the divine messages only after they had already been received—this for our benefit, so that we might hear in human language. This also made clear who were the hypocrites and non believers by giving them the occasion to deny, as they would not believe in angels.

The proof that the Holy Qur'ān was revealed directly to the Prophet ﷺ is in the Qur'ān itself.

> *And thou art surely made to receive the Qur'ān from the All-Wise, the All-Knowing.* (Sūra Naml, 6)

Since the Prophet ﷺ received revelation before the angel Gabriel brought it to him, each time Gabriel عليه السلام delivered the holy verses, the Prophet ﷺ found them in his heart and recited them before they were given. That is the reason for the verse:

> *And make not haste with the Qur'ān before its revelation is made complete to thee...* (Sūra Ṭā Hā, 114)

This situation is made clear by the fact that when Gabriel عليه السلام accompanied the Prophet ﷺ on the night of his ascension, he could not go any further than the seventh heaven, and saying, 'If I take another step I will burn to ashes', he left our Master ﷺ to continue on his own.

Allah describes the blessed olive tree, the tree of unity, as being neither of the East nor of the West. In other words, it has neither a beginning nor an end, and the light of which it is the source has no rising or setting. It is eternal in the past and never-ending in the future. Both Allah's Essence and His attributes are ever-existent, because His attributes are light generated from His Essence. Both the manifestation of His Essence and the manifestation of His attributes are dependent on His Essence.

True worship can only be performed when the veils hiding the heart are lifted so that that eternal light shines upon it. It is only then that the heart is enlightened by the divine light. It is only then that the soul sees the truth through that celestial niche.

The purpose of the creation of this universe is to discover, to see that hidden treasure. Allah says through His Prophet ﷺ, 'I was a hidden treasure, I willed to be known. I created the creation so that I would be known.' That is to say, that He would be known in this material world through His attributes manifested in His creation. But to see His very Essence is left to the hereafter. There, the vision of Allah will be direct, as He wills, and it will be the eye of the child of the heart that sees Him.

> *On that day some faces will beam* (with joy and beauty), *looking at their Lord.* (Sūra Qiyāma, 22–3)

Our Master the Prophet ﷺ says, 'I have seen my Lord in the shape of a beautiful youth.' Perhaps this is the manifestation of the child of the heart. The image is the mirror. It becomes a means, rendering visible that which is invisible. The truth of Allah Most High is exempt from and free of any kind of description or any kind of image or form. The image is the mirror, though what is seen is neither the mirror nor the one who is looking into the mirror. Ponder on that and try to understand, because that is the essence of the realm of secrets.

Yet all this is happening in this world of attributes. In the realm of the Essence all means disappear, burn into thin air. The ones in that realm of Essence themselves do not exist, but they feel the Essence and nothing else. How well the Prophet ﷺ explains this when he says, 'I knew my Lord by my Lord'. In His Light, by His Light! The truth of man is the secret of that light, as Allah says through His Prophet: 'Man is My secret and I am his secret'.

The place of the Prophet Muḥammad ﷺ, whose light is the first of Allah's creation, is described in his own words, 'I am from Allah and the believers are from me'. And Allah, speaking through His Prophet ﷺ, says: 'I have created the light of Muḥammad from the light of my own existence'. The meaning of Allah's own existence is His divine Essence manifested in His attribute of the Most Compassionate. This He declares through His Prophet ﷺ, saying: 'My compassion far surpasses My punishment'. The beloved Messenger of Allah ﷺ is the light of the Truth, for Allah says, *We sent thee not but as a mercy to the whole creation.* (Sūra Anbiyā', 107) and

> *Indeed Our Messenger has come to you, making clear to you much of that which you concealed of the Book and passing over much. Indeed, there has come to you from Allah a light...* (Sūra Mā'ida, 15)

The importance of the beloved Prophet of Allah is made clear when Allah speaks to him and says: 'But for you, I would not have created creation'.

CHAPTER TEN

The Veils of Light and Darkness

ALLAH says: *Whoever is blind in this world, he will be blind in the hereafter.* (Sūra Banī Isrā'īl, 72) it is not the blindness of the eyes in one's head but the blindness of the eyes of one's heart that will prevent one from seeing the light of the hereafter. As Allah says: *For surely it is not their eyes that are blind, but their hearts which are in their breasts.* (Sūra Ḥajj, 46) The only cause of the heart becoming blind is heedlessness, which makes one forget Allah and one's function, one's purpose, one's promise to Him, while one is in this world. The principal cause of heedlessness is ignorance of the reality of the divine laws and orders. What keeps one in this stage of ignorance is a darkness that completely covers one from the outside and fully invades one's inner being. Some of the properties of this darkness are arrogance, pride, envy, miserliness, vengeance, lying, gossiping, backbiting and so many other hateful traits. It is these traits that reduce the best creation of Allah to the lowest of the low.

To rid oneself of these evils one has to cleanse and shine the mirror of the heart. This cleansing is done by acquiring knowledge, by acting upon this knowledge, by effort and valour, fighting against one's ego within and without oneself, by ridding oneself of one's multiplicity of being, by achieving unity. This struggle will continue until the heart becomes alive with the light of unity—and with that light of unity, the eye of the clean heart will see the reality of Allah's attributes around and in it.

Only then will you remember the true home from which you come. Then you will have the yearning and longing to return to the true home, and when the time comes, with the help of the Most Compassionate, that spirit which is pure in you will go to join Him.

When the attributes of darkness lift, light takes its place, and the one with the eye of the soul sees. He recognizes what he sees with the light of the Names of divine attributes. Then he himself is flooded by light and becomes light. These lights are still veils hiding the light of the divine Essence, but the time comes when they too are drawn back, leaving only the light of the divine Essence itself.

The heart has two eyes, one lesser, the other greater. With the lesser eye one may be able to see the manifestation of Allah's attributes and Names. This vision continues all through one's spiritual evolution. The greater eye sees only that which is rendered visible by the light of unity and oneness. Only when one comes to the regions of Allah's intimacy does it see, in the ultimate realm of the manifestation of Allah's Essence, the unity of the Absolute.

In order to reach these levels on this earth in this life you must cleanse yourself from your worldly attributes, which are egoistic and egotistical. The distance you must travel in your ascent towards these levels depends on the distance that you have put between yourself and the low desires of your flesh and your ego.

Your attainment of the goal you wish for is not like a material thing's arriving at a material place. Neither is it like knowledge leading one to a thing that becomes known, nor like reason obtaining that which is rational, nor like the imagination joining with that which it fancies. The goal that you wish to attain is the realization of your emptiness of all else except the Essence of Allah. This attainment is a becoming. There is no distance, nor closeness nor farness, nor reaching, nor measure, nor direction, nor dimension.

He is All-glorious, all praise is due to Him, He is Most Merciful. He becomes visible in what He hides from you. He manifests Himself as He puts veils between Himself and you. His being known is hidden in His not being known.

If any of you reach that light which is suggested in this book while you are here in this world, try to balance your book of deeds. It is only under light that you can see what you have done, what you are doing; do your accounting, make it balance. You will have to read your book in front of your Lord on the day of Last Judgment. That is final. You will not then have the chance to balance it. If you do that here, while you have the time, you will be of those who are saved. Otherwise pain and disaster is your lot in this world and in the hereafter. This life will end. There is the pain of the grave, there is the day of Last Judgment, there is the balance that will weigh the smallest sin and the tiniest of good deeds. Then there is the test of that bridge, thinner than a hair and sharper than a sword, at the end of which is the Garden, under which is the Fire and so much hardship, and for so long, when this short life ends.

CHAPTER ELEVEN

The Joy of Being Good and the Misery of the Rebel

YOU should know that all men are included in one or another of two classes: the class of people who are at peace, content and happy, doing good deeds in a state of obedience to Allah, and those who are in a state of insecurity, doubt and misery in their rebellion against the prescriptions of Allah. Both the quality of obedience and that of rebelliousness are present in each human being. If the purity, the sincerity and the good in one are dominant, one's selfish characteristics are transformed into spiritual states and one's rebellious side is overcome by one's good side. On the other hand, if one follows the low desires of one's flesh and the tendencies of one's ego, one's rebellious character dominates that which is selfless and obedient in one, and one becomes a rebel. If both of these contrary characteristics are equal, the hope is that the good will overcome, as is promised: *He that doeth good shall have ten times as much to his credit...* (Sūra An'ām, 160) And if Allah so wishes, He may even further increase His favours.

Yet that person in whom evil and good are equal will still have to pass the terrible trial of the day of the Last Judgment, while for the one who was able to transform his selfishness into selflessness, the low desires of his flesh into spiritual aspirations, there will be no trial, there is no accounting to be given. He will enter Paradise without passing through the terrors of the Last Day.

> *Then he whose balance* (of good deeds) *will be found heavy will be in a life of good pleasure and satisfaction.* (Sūra Qāri'a, 6–7)

For the one whose errors are heavier than his good deeds there will be punishment in proportion to the amount of his crimes, after which he will be taken out of hellfire and, if he has faith, will enter Paradise.

Obedience and rebelliousness mean good and evil. These are present in every man, yet they do not stay as they are. The good may turn into evil and the evil into good, as our Master the Prophet ﷺ says: 'While the one in whom good is dominant finds salvation, peace and joy, and becomes good, and the one in whom evil is more than good rebels and becomes evil, the one who recognizes his errors and repents and changes his ways will have his state of rebelliousness transformed into obedience and devotion.'

It is indeed decreed that both good and evil, both the blissful life of the obedient believer and the miserable life of the rebel, are states that people are born with. Both are hidden in the potential of every man. Our Master the Prophet ﷺ says, 'The one who is fortunate enough to be good is good in his mother's womb, and the wretched sinner is a sinner already in his mother's womb.' That is the way it is, and no one has the right to discuss it. The matter of destiny is not to be discussed, for if one is led to such discussion one is led to heresy and disbelief.

Furthermore, no one has the right to use destiny as an argument to abandon all effort, all good deeds. One may not say, 'If my destiny is to be one of the good, why should I tire myself trying to do good deeds, as I am already blessed?' or, 'If it is my destiny to be evil, what good will it do to be good?' Obviously this is not right. It is not proper to say, 'If my state is fixed from my past, what benefit or loss can I hope for with my efforts in the present?' The best example given to us is the comparison of the first man and prophet, Adam عليه السلام with the accursed Devil. The Devil put the blame for his revolt on his destiny and became an infidel and was rejected from the mercy and presence of His Lord. Adam عليه السلام admitted his fault. Assuming the responsibility for his error, he asked forgiveness, received Allah's mercy, and was saved.

It is incumbent upon all believers and all Muslims not to try to understand the causes of the unfolding of destiny. Whoever does this will become confused and will gain nothing but doubt. He may even lose his faith. The faithful must believe in Allah's absolute wisdom. Everything that man sees happening in himself and in this world certainly has a cause, but that cause is not to be understood by human logic, as it is based on divine wisdom. In the life of this world, when you encounter blasphemy, hypocrisy, duplicity and all other things that seem to be evil, let these things not shake your faith. Know that Allah Most High in His absolute wisdom is responsible for all and everything, and He does what appears to be negative in order to express His infinite power. Manifestation of such overwhelming power may seem to some unbearable, and therefore negative, but there is great mystery in this that no one other than our Prophet ﷺ could know.

There is a story of a wise man who prayed to his Lord, saying, 'O Divine One, all is preordained by You. My fate is Yours, the will is Yours, the wisdom which You put in me is Your creation!'

As he prayed, he heard a response without sound, without words, coming from inside him, which said, 'O My servant, all that you say belongs to the One Who is unique and united. It does not belong to the servant.'

The believing servant said, 'O my Lord, I have tyrannized myself, I am in error, I have sinned!'

After that confession he again heard the voice from within him: 'And I have had mercy upon you, I have erased your faults, I have forgiven you.'

Let the ones who have faith know and be thankful that all the good they do is not from them but through them. Success comes from the Creator. When they err, let them know that their mistakes and their sins belong to them, that they may repent. Wrong comes from the unjustified ambitions of their egos. If you understand this and follow it, you belong to the ones who are mentioned by Allah as:

> *Those who, having done something to be ashamed of, or who have wronged their own souls, earnestly bring Allah to mind and ask for forgiveness for their sins—and who can forgive sins except Allah?—and are never obstinate in persisting knowingly in* (the wrong) *they have done, for such the reward is forgiveness from their Lord and gardens with rivers flowing underneath—an eternal dwelling...* (Sūra Āl 'Imrān, 135–136)

It is better for the believer to accept that he himself is the source of all of his own faults. That is what will save him. It indeed is much better than attributing his faults to the Almighty and Powerful, the One who created all.

When our Master said, 'It is already known when one is in the mother's womb whether one will be a sinner or be righteous,' he meant by 'the mother's womb' the four elements that give birth to all material forces and faculties. Two of these four elements are earth and water, which are responsible for the growth of faith and of knowledge, give life to the living, and appear in the heart as humbleness, for earth is humble. The other two elements are fire and ether. They are the opposite of earth and water. They burn, destroy, kill. It is the Divine that unites these opposites in one being. How do water and fire coexist? How are light and darkness contained within the clouds?

> *It is He Who shows you lightning, causing both fear and hope; it is He Who raises up the clouds heavy with rain.*
>
> *Nay, thunder repeats His praises and so do the angels, with awe. He flings the loud-voiced thunderbolts and therewith strikes whomsoever He will...* (Sūra Ra'd, 12,13)

One day someone asked the saint Yaḥyā ibn Mu'ādh al-Rāzī, 'How did you come to know Allah?' He answered, 'By the union of opposites.'

The opposites pertain to, and in fact are a requirement for, the understanding of Allah's attributes. Facing the divine truth man becomes the mirror in which the truth is reflected, but also in which the attribute of Might is reflected. Man contains the whole universe in his being: that is why he is called the unifier of multiplicity, the macrocosm. Allah has created him with His two hands, His hand of grace and His hand of all-compelling, crushing power and wrath. Therefore he is a mirror that shows both sides, both that which is coarse and dense and that which is fine and exquisite.

While all the divine Names are manifested in man, all other creations are only one-sided. Allah created the accursed Devil and his progeny from His attribute of all-compelling wrath. He created the angels from His attribute of grace. The qualities of sanctity and continuous worship are contained in the angels, while the Devil and his followers, created from Allah's attribute of crushing wrath, have the quality of tyranny. That is why the Devil became arrogant and, when ordered by Allah to prostrate himself to Adam, refused.

As man contains in himself both the high and low characteristics of the universe, and as Allah has chosen His messengers and saints from among men, these messengers are not free from error either. Prophets when they receive the mission of prophethood are made innocent of great sins, but the small sins and errors may still be manifested in them. The saints, on the other hand, are not rendered incapable of sins. Yet it is said that when saints who come close to Allah reach perfection, they come under divine protection against committing great sins.

Shaqīq al-Balkhī, may Allah sanctify his secret, says, 'There are five signs of righteousness: a gentle disposition and a soft heart, shedding tears of regret, asceticism and not caring about the world, being unambitious, and having a conscience. The signs of a sinner are also five: to be hard-hearted, to have eyes that never cry, to love the world and the worldly, to be ambitious, and to be without conscience and shame.'

The Prophet ﷺ attributes four qualities to the righteous person: 'He is dependable and safeguards that which is given into his care, and returns it. He keeps his promises. He is truthful and never lies. He is not harsh in discussion and does not break hearts.' He also mentions four signs of the sinner: 'He is unfaithful and un-dependable and careless with things entrusted to his care. He does not keep his promises. He lies. He fights and curses as he discusses and he breaks hearts.' Moreover, the sinner is unable to forgive the errors of his friends. This is a sign of faithlessness, just as to forgive is the greatest sign of the believer, for Allah Most High Himself ordered His beloved Prophet ﷺ: *Hold to forgiveness, command what is right, but turn away from the ignorant.* (Sūra A'rāf, 199)

The order, 'Hold to forgiveness' is not given only to our Master the Prophet. It addresses everyone, and certainly all people who believe in Muḥammad ﷺ. If a king orders his governor to do a certain thing, abiding with that order becomes incumbent upon everyone under that governor, even though the order itself was given only to him.

In the order, 'Hold to forgiveness,' the word 'hold' means 'Make it a habit, make it a part of your nature, a part of yourself.' Whoever has a forgiving nature receives one of Allah's Names, the Name of the Forgiver. Allah promises, *If a person forgives and makes reconciliation, his reward is due from Allah...* (Sūra Shūrā, 40) Know that righteousness turns into rebellion against Allah, and rebellion and sin into righteousness, not by themselves, but through influences and by one's own doing and effort. As our Prophet says, 'All children are born as Muslims. It is their mothers and fathers that turn them into Jews, Christians or Magian fire-worshippers.' Everyone has the potential of being good and of being bad. Therefore is it wrong to judge someone or something as totally good or totally bad. It is right to think that if someone has more good in him than he has bad, he is righteous, and if his bad features are more than the good, the reverse.

This does not mean that man gains Paradise without good deeds, nor does it mean that he is thrown into hellfire without sins. To think this way is in opposition to the principles of Islam. Allah has promised Paradise to His believing servants who do good deeds, and has warned the rebelling, non-believing sinners who set themselves up as partners to Him with the punishment of hellfire. He said,

Whoever does good, it is for himself, and whoever does evil, it is against himself. Then to your Lord you will be brought back. (Sūra Jāthiya, 15)

This day everyone is rewarded with what he has earned. No in justice this day! Surely Allah is swift in reckoning. (Sūra Mu'min, 17)

Man can have nothing but what he strives for. (Sūra Najm, 39)

And whatever good you send before for yourselves, you will find it with Allah. (Sūra Baqara, 110)

CHAPTER TWELVE

The Dervishes

THERE is a group of people called the Sufis. Four interpretations are given for this name. Some see, looking at their exterior, that they wear rough woollen garb. In Arabic the word for wool is *ṣūf*, and they call them Sufis from this. Others, looking at their way of life free from the anxieties of this world, and at their ease and at peace, which in Arabic is *ṣafā*, call them Sufis on that account. Yet others, seeing deeper, look at their hearts, which are purified of everything other than the Essence of Allah. Because of the purity of those hearts, in Arabic *ṣāfī*, they term them Sufis. Others who know call them Sufis because they are close to Allah and will stand in the first row, in Arabic *ṣaff*, before Allah on the day of the Last Judgment.

There are also four realms, four worlds. The first is the world of matter, of earth, water, fire and ether. The second is the world of spiritual beings, of the angels, of jinns and dreams and death, of the rewards of Allah—the eight paradises, and the justice of Allah—the seven hells. The third is the world of the Word, the Beautiful Names of Allah's attributes, and the Hidden Tablet which is the source of all of Allah's messages. The fourth is the realm of Allah's pure Essence, a realm indescribable because at that level there are no words, names, attributes or likenesses. None except Allah knows it.

There are also four kinds of knowledge. The first is knowledge of Allah's precepts, and is concerned with the outer aspects of the life of this world. The second is mystical knowledge, the inner knowledge of causes and effects. The third is the knowledge of the spirit, self-knowledge, and through it, knowledge of the divine. Finally, there is the knowledge of the truth.

The souls are also of four kinds: the material soul, the enlightened soul, the sultan-soul and the divine soul.

Appearances, the manifestations of the Creator, are also of four kinds. The first is the manifestation in forms and shapes and colour, as if in His artwork. The second manifestation is in actions and interactions, in things that happen. The third is His manifestation in attributes, qualities, the character of things. Finally there is the manifestation of His Essence.

The intellect, or reasoning power, is also of four kinds: the intelligence which deals with worldly affairs of this life; the intelligence which considers and thinks of the hereafter; the intelligence of the soul, spiritual wisdom; and finally the total Causal Mind.

The subjects just discussed are also four: the four kinds of knowledge, the four souls, the four kinds of manifestation and the four intellects. Some men stay at the first level of knowledge, soul, manifestation and intellect. They are the inhabitants of the first paradise called 'the paradise of the security of home', that is, the earthly paradise. Those who are at the second level of knowledge, soul, manifestation and intellect belong to a higher level of Paradise, the garden of the delight of Allah's grace upon His creatures, which is the paradise within the angelic realm. Those among men who have reached the third level of knowledge, soul, manifestation and wisdom are in the third level of Paradise, the heavenly paradise, the paradise of the divine Names and attributes in the realm of unity.

Yet those who seek and attach themselves to the rewards of Allah, even if they are in Paradise, cannot see the true reality within themselves and within the things around them. Those men of wisdom who seek the truth, those who have achieved the true state of the dervish, the state of total need—not the need of anything but

Allah, the need of Allah alone—leave everything and seek nothing but truth. They find what they seek and enter the realm of truth, the realm which is closest to Allah, and live for nothing except the Essence of Allah.

These abide with the divine order, 'Take refuge in Allah', and follow the advice of the Prophet ﷺ, 'Both this world and the hereafter are unlawful for the one who seeks Allah'. Our Master does not mean that the world and the hereafter are unlawful. He means that the ones who wish for and seek Allah's Essence deprive their flesh and their egos of their needs, loves and demands of the world and the worldly.

The seekers of truth reason this way: this world is a created being; we are also created beings, we are both in need of a Creator, of an Owner. How could one in need ask for what he needs from another who is in need himself? What way is there for a created being other than seeking his Creator?

Allah says through the lips of His beloved Prophet ﷺ, 'My love, My existence is their love for Me'.

Our Master the Prophet ﷺ says: 'My state of utter need, my poverty, is my pride.' The utter need and love of Allah is the basis for the search of the dervish. The state of poverty which is the pride of our Master is not the poverty of the lack of the worldly. It is the abandonment of everything but the wish for the Essence of Allah. It is to leave all the goods—not only those of this world, but those promised in the hereafter—and thus in total need to present oneself to one's Lord.

This is a state of bringing oneself to nothingness, of disappearing in the Essence of Allah. It is to empty one's being of everything which is for one's being and to empty one's heart of everything but His love. Then that heart becomes worthy to receive the promise of Allah, 'I do not fit into My heavens nor My earths, but I fit into the heart of my faithful servant'.

The faithful servant is he who excludes all other than the One from his heart. When a heart is thus purified, Allah enlarges it and fits Himself into it. Ḥaḍrat Bāyazīd al-Bistāmī, may Allah sanctity his secret, describes the greatness of such a heart, saying, 'If all that exists in and around the Throne of Allah, that vastest of all of Allah's creations, were to be placed in a comer of the perfect man's heart, he would not even feel the weight of it.'

Such as these are the beloved of Allah. Love them and be around them, for those who truly love will be with their beloved in the hereafter. The sign of this love is to seek their company, to wish to hear their words, and with their sight and their words to feel longing for Allah Most High.

Allah, speaking through the lips of His Prophet ﷺ says: 'I feel the yearning of the faithful, of the righteous, of the true servants, for Me, and I too long for them.'

These lovers of Allah appear different from others, and their actions are different from those of others. At the beginning, when they are novices, their actions appear balanced between good and bad. When they are advanced and reach the median level their actions are full of beneficence. In all cases the good which comes through them is not only in their following the precepts of Allah and of the religion, but in actions which contain beatitude and shine with the light of the meaning within appearances.

They are as if clad in clothing of coloured light which generates from them in accordance with their levels.

As they overcome their egos and the tyranny of the lower desires of their flesh with the blessing of the divine phrase LĀ ILĀHA ILLĀ LLĀH—there is no god but Allah—and reach the level of beings who can discriminate between right and wrong, condemn the wrong within themselves and wish for the right, a sky-blue light emanates from them.

When, from that state, with the help and inspiration of ALLĀH they opt for the good and leave the bad, a red colour engulfs them.

With the blessing coming from the Name of Allah, HŪ, that Name which none other than the Truth can describe, they reach the level that is cleansed of all harmful attributes and bad actions and find a state of peace and serenity. Then a green light emanates from them.

When all ego and its wishes, when all personal will is left behind through the blessing of ḤAQQ, the Truth, and when they submit their wills to the will of Allah and are pleased with all that comes from Allah, their colour turns to white light.

These are the descriptions of dervishes from their novitiate at the beginning of the path until they reach a median stage. But the one who reaches the limits of this path has neither form nor shape nor colour. He becomes as if a ray of sunshine. The sunshine is colourless. Its light does not resemble any colour. The dervish who has reached the highest level has no being to reflect light or colour. If anything, his colour would be black, which absorbs all light. This is the sign of the state of annihilation.

For others who look at him, this colourless, dark appearance becomes a veil over the light of wisdom which he possesses, just as the night is a veil over the sunshine. Allah says that He

> *made the night as a covering, and made the day as a means of subsistence.* (Sūra Nabā', 10–11)

For those who have reached the essence of the mind and of knowledge, there is a sign in this verse.

Those people who have come close to truth in the life of this world feel as if they are imprisoned here in a dark dungeon. They spend their life in pain and misery. They suffer great hardships, pressure of circumstances, in a world of total darkness. The Prophet ﷺ says, 'This world is a dungeon for the faithful'. As he points out, calamities fall first upon the prophets, then upon those who are the closest to Allah, then in descending scale upon those who are trying to come close to Him. Therefore it is appropriate for the dervish to wear black and to tie the black turban around his head, for it is the clothing of the one who is prepared to suffer the pains of this path.

In reality, black is the appropriate clothing for those who should mourn for having lost their humanity and their possibility. Many men carelessly lose that great gift, proper only to mankind, of being conscious, of being able to see the truth, thus killing with their own hands their eternal life. Putting out the divine love yearning in their hearts, separating themselves from the holy spirit, they lose the possibility of returning to the origin, to the cause. Although they do not know it, they are the ones who suffer the greatest of calamities. If they were aware that they had lost all the benefits of the hereafter, the eternal life, they would indeed wear the clothing of mourning. A widow who has lost her husband mourns for four months and ten days. This is a mourning for the loss of that which belongs to this world. The mourning for the one who has lost the good of the eternal life should be eternal.

Our Master the Prophet ﷺ says: 'Those who are sincere are always at the edge of a great danger'. How well this description fits the one who has to walk on tiptoe with the greatest of care! But this is the state of the dervish who has left his being and is in the realm of annihilation. His poverty of this world which he has left behind and his total need for Allah is great, and he looms as a great beauty over and above humankind.

Our Master says, 'Poverty is a blackened face in both worlds'. He means that the one who has purposefully chosen to be poor in this world, disappearing to this world, does not reflect any of the colours of this world, but absorbs only the light of the divine truth. The dark of his face is like a beauty spot which further enhances his beauty.

Those who have come in sight of the truth, after beholding the beauty of the truth, do not care to see anything else. They cannot look with love and yearning at anything else. For them Allah becomes the only beloved, the only thing that exists. That is their state in both worlds. That is their only purpose. Finally, they have become Men, and Allah has created Man in order that he know Him, in order that he reach His Essence.

It behoves all men to seek and know the reason for their creation and to feel the meaning of this reason, the duties which befall them in this world and in the hereafter, so that they do not spend their life here in vain, so that they do not regret forever in the hereafter—engulfed, drowned in the yearning which they will finally realize in eternal remorse.

CHAPTER THIRTEEN

On the Purification of the Self

PURIFICATION is cleansing oneself. There are two kinds of cleanliness. One, exterior, is ordained by the precepts of the religion and is carried out by washing one's body with pure water. The other, inner purification, is obtained through the realization of the dirt in one's being, being aware of one's sins and sincerely repenting for them. This inner purification necessitates taking a spiritual path and is taught by a spiritual teacher.

According to the religious rules and precepts, one becomes impure and one's ablution is broken when certain bodily matter such as faeces, urine, vomit, pus, blood, semen, etc., is expelled. This necessitates the renewal of the ablution. In the case of semen and menstrual bleeding a total washing of the body is necessary. In other cases the exposed extremities of the body—the hands and forearms, the face and feet—must be washed. Concerning renewing one's ablution our Master the Prophet ﷺ said: 'At each renewal of ablution Allah renews the belief of His servant whose light of faith is repolished and shines brighter,' and 'Repeated purification by ablution is light upon light'.

Inner purity can also be lost, perhaps more often than outer purity, by bad character, low behaviour, harmful acts and attitudes such as pride, arrogance, lying, gossiping, slandering, envy and anger. Conscious and unconscious acts by one's senses soil the spirit: the mouth which eats unlawful food, the lips which lie and curse, the ear which listens to gossip and slander, the hand which strikes, the feet which follow the tyrant. Adultery, which is also a sin, is not performed only in bed; as the Prophet ﷺ says, 'The eyes also commit adultery'.

When inner purity is thus soiled and spiritual ablution broken, the renewal of ablution is by sincere repentance, which is performed by realizing one's fault, by painful regret accompanied by tears (which are the water washing the dirt from the spirit), by intending never to repeat this fault, by wishing to leave all faults, by asking the forgiveness of Allah, and by praying that He prevent one from committing such a sin again.

To pray is to present oneself in front of one's Lord. To have ablution, to be in a purified state, is a prerequisite for prayer. The wise know that the cleanliness of one's exterior being is not sufficient, for Allah sees deep into one's heart, which has to be given the ablution of repentance. Only then is prayer accepted. Allah says

> *This is what was promised for you—for every one who turned* (to Allah) *in sincere repentance, who kept* (His law). (Sūra Qāf, 32)

The purification of the body and exterior ablution in accordance with religious precepts is also bound by time, for sleep cancels ablution as well. This cleanliness is tied to the day and the night of the life of this world. The cleanliness of the inner world, the ablution of the invisible self, is not limited by time. It is for the whole of life—not only for the temporal life of this world, but also for the eternal life of the hereafter.

CHAPTER FOURTEEN

On the Meaning of Ritual Worship and Inner Worship

FIVE times a day, at specific times, prayer is ordained for every adult and able Muslim. This is ordered by Allah: *Guard the prayers, especially the middle prayer...* (Sūra Baqara, 238) Ritual worship consists of standing, reciting from the Qur'ān, bowing, prostrating, kneeling and audibly repeating certain prayers. These movements and actions involving the members of the body, recitations spelled out and heard involving the senses, are the worship of the material self. Because these actions of the material self are multiple and are repeated many times in each of the five prayers during the day, the first part of the order of Allah, *Guard the prayers*, is in the plural.

The second part of Allah's order, *especially the middle prayer*, refers to the prayer of the heart, because the heart is in the middle, in the centre of the being. The purpose of that worship is to obtain peace of heart. The heart is in the middle between the right and the left, between the front and the back, between the upper and the lower, and between righteousness and rebellion. The heart is the centre, the point of balance, the median. Our Master the Prophet ﷺ said, 'The hearts of the children of Adam are between the two fingers of the All-Merciful. He turns them whichever way He wills.' The two fingers of Allah are His attributes of the irresistible power of punishment and the loving and delicate beauty of beneficence.

True worship is the worship of the heart. If one's heart is heedless of true worship, the ritual prayer of the material self is in disorder. When this happens, the peace of the material self that one hopes to obtain from ritual prayer is not realized. That is why the Prophet ﷺ says, 'Ritual worship is only possible with a quiet heart'.

Prayer is the supplication of the created to the Creator. It is a meeting of the servant and the Lord. The place of this meeting is the heart. If the heart is closed, heedless, and dead, so is the meaning of worship. No good comes to the material being from such a prayer. For the heart is the essence of the body; the rest is dependent upon it. As the Prophet ﷺ says, 'There is a piece of meat in man's body—when it is in a good state, the whole being improves, and when it is in a bad state, the whole being falls apart. Beware, that piece of meat is the heart.'

Prayer prescribed by the religion is to be performed at specific times. Within a day and a night there are five such specific times of prayer. The best way of doing them is to perform them in a mosque, in congregation, turning toward the direction of the city of Makka, following the one who leads the prayer without hypocrisy, not for the approval of others, and without ostentation.

The time for inner worship is timeless and endless, for the whole life here and in the hereafter. The mosque for this prayer is the heart. The congregation is the inner faculties, which remember and recite the Names of the unity of Allah in the language of the inner world. The leader of this prayer is the irresistible wish. The direction of prayer is toward the oneness of Allah—which is everywhere—and His eternal nature and His beauty.

The true heart is the one which can perform such a prayer. A heart like this neither sleeps nor dies. A heart and soul like this are in continuous worship, and a being with such a heart, whether he appear awake or asleep, is in constant service. The inner worship of the heart is his whole life. There is no longer the sound of recitation nor standing, bowing, prostrating or sitting. His guide, the leader of his prayer, is the Prophet ﷺ himself. He speaks with Allah Most High, saying, *Thee do we serve and Thee do we beseech for help.* (Sūra Fātiḥa, 4) These divine words are interpreted as a sign of the state of the perfect man, who passes from being nothing, being lost to material things, into a state of oneness. Such a perfect heart receives great blessings from the divine. One of these blessings is mentioned by our Master the Prophet ﷺ: 'The prophets and those who are beloved by Allah continue their worship in their graves as they did in their houses while they were of this world.' In other words, the eternal life of the heart continues its supplications to Allah Most High.

When the ritual worship of the material being and the inner worship of the heart unite, the prayer is complete. It is perfect worship, and its rewards are great. It brings one spiritually to the realms of the proximity of Allah, and physically to the highest level of one's possibility. In the world of appearances one becomes the devout servant of Allah. Inwardly one becomes the wise one who has attained the true knowledge of Allah. If ritual worship does not unite with the inner worship of the heart, it is lacking. Its reward is only advancing in rank. It will not bring one any closer to the realm of the divine.

CHAPTER FIFTEEN

On the Purification of the Perfect Man, who has Isolated Himself from, and Stripped Himself of, All Worldly Concerns

THE purpose of this purification is of two kinds: one is to gain access to the divine attributes, and the other is to reach the realm of the Essence.

Purification to gain access to divine attributes necessitates a teaching that will instruct one in the process of cleansing the mirror of the heart from animal and human images by the invocation of the divine Names. This invocation becomes the key, the password opening the eye of the heart. Only when that eye is opened can one see the true attributes of Allah Most High. Then that eye sees the reflection of the divine mercy, grace, beauty and kindness on the purified mirror of the heart. The Prophet of Allah ﷺ says, 'The faithful sees by the light of Allah', and 'The faithful is the mirror of the faithful'. He also says, 'The man of knowledge makes images while the wise man polishes the mirror upon which truth is reflected'. When the mirror of the heart is completely cleansed by being polished with continuous invocation of the divine Names, one has access to and knowledge of the divine attributes. The witnessing of this vision is only possible in the mirror of the heart.

Purification for the purpose of attaining the divine Essence is through continuous remembrance and the invocation of the

Confession of Unity. There are three Names of Unity, the last three of the twelve divine Names. They are:

LĀ ILĀHA ILLĀ LLĀH—There is no god but Allah
ALLĀH—The proper name of God
HŪ—The transcendent Allah
ḤAQQ—The Truth
ḤAYY—The everliving divine Life
QAYYŪM—The Self-existing One upon Whom all existence depends
QAHHĀR—The All-compeller Who overwhelms all
WAHHĀB—The limitless Donor of all
FATTĀḤ—The Opener
WĀḤID—The One
AḤAD—The Unique
ṢAMAD—The Source

These Names must be invoked not by the ordinary tongue, but with the secret tongue of the heart. It is only then that the eye of the heart sees the light of unity. When the sacred light of the divine Essence becomes manifest, all material qualities disappear, all things become nothing. This is the state of total consumption of all and everything, a void beyond all voids. The manifestation of divine light extinguishes all other lights.

> *Everything will perish but Him.* (Sūra Qaṣaṣ, 88)

> *Allah effaces what He pleases and establishes what He pleases, and His is the essence of the Book.* (Sūra Ra'd, 39)

When all is gone, what is left forever is the holy spirit. It sees with the light of Allah. It sees Him, He sees it. It sees by Him; it sees in Him; it sees for Him. There are no images, no likenesses in His seeing. *Nothing is like Him, and He is the Hearing and the Seeing.* (Sūra Shūrā, 11)

What is left is a pure and absolute light. There is nothing to know beyond it. That is the realm of self-annihilation. There is no longer a mind to give any news. There is no one else but Allah to whom to give news. Our Master the Prophet ﷺ describes it, saying, 'I have a time when I am so close to Allah that no one, neither an angel nor a messenger nor a prophet, can come between us.' That is the state of isolation, where one has stripped oneself of everything except Allah's Essence. That is the state of union, as Allah ordains from the lips of His Prophet ﷺ, 'isolate yourself from all and find union'.

The isolation proceeds from all that is worldly becoming nothing. It is only then that you will receive the divine attributes. That is what our Master the Prophet ﷺ means when he says, 'Adorn yourself with the divine disposition'. Purify yourself, submerging yourself in the divine attributes.

CHAPTER SIXTEEN

On Charity

THERE are two kinds of charity: that charity which is prescribed by the religion, and spiritual charity, which is of a different nature. The donations prescribed by the religion are from the lawfully gained goods of this world. After the deduction of a certain amount allocated for the use of one's family, a specific percentage of the excess is distributed to those who are in need. Spiritual charity, however, is taken from that which one has obtained of the goods of the hereafter. It also is given to the ones who are in need of it, to the spiritually poor.

Charity is giving alms to the poor. Allah ordains this, saying, *Charity is for the poor and the needy...* (Sūra Tawba, 60) Whatever is given for this purpose passes through the hands of Allah Most High before it reaches the one in need. Therefore the purpose of charity is not so much to help the needy, for Allah is the Satisfier of all needs, but to let the donor's intentions be acceptable to Allah.

Those who are close to Allah devote the spiritual rewards of their good deeds to sinners. Allah Most High manifests His mercy, pardoning sinners, in proportion to the prayers, the praises, the fasts, the alms and the pilgrimages of His servants who intend to sacrifice the spiritual rewards they may hope for as a result of their worship and devotions. Allah in His mercy covers and hides the sins of sinners as a reward for the devotion of his good servants.

The generosity of these faithful ones is such that they keep nothing for themselves, neither the reputation of being good nor the hope of a reward in the hereafter. For the one who takes this path has lost even his own existence. He is in the state of total bankruptcy, because he is truly generous. Allah loves those who are generous up to the point of being totally bankrupt to this world. Our Master the Prophet ﷺ says, 'The one who has spent all he has and does not hope to have anything is in the care of Allah in this world and in the hereafter.'

The great lady Rābi'a al-'Adawiyya, may God be pleased with her, used to pray, begging Allah, 'O Lord, give all my share of this world to the non believers, and if I have any share of the hereafter, distribute it among Your faithful servants. All I wish for in this world is to yearn for You, and all I wish for in the hereafter is to be with You; for both man and what comes to his hands for a short while belong only to the Owner of both.'

Allah repays at least ten times to the ones who give. *He who does good shall have ten times as much in return...* (Sūra An'ām, 160)

Another benefit of charity is its cleansing effect. It cleanses one's property and it cleanses one's being. If one's being is cleansed of egotistical attributes, the spiritual purpose of charity is accomplished.

To separate oneself from a little portion of what one thinks is one's own brings manifold rewards in the hereafter. Allah promises:

> *Who is he who will give to Allah a beautiful gift? For Allah will increase it manifold to his credit, and he will have besides a liberal reward.* (Sūra Ḥadīd, 11)

and *Truly he finds salvation who purifies* (his soul). (Sūra Shams, 9)

Charity, the 'beautiful gift,' is a good deed, a portion of what you have received, both material and spiritual. Give it, for Allah's sake, to Allah's servants. Even though manifold rewards are promised, do not do it for the return. Give all gifts and charity accompanied by care, love, and compassion and not as a favour, expecting thanks, making the recipient feel under obligation, indebted or grateful. For Allah says:

> *O you who believe, make not your charity worthless by reminders of your generosity, and by causing vexation. . .* (Sūra Baqara, 264)

Do not ask nor expect any worldly benefit for your good deeds. Do them for Allah's sake. Allah says,

> *By no means shall you attain righteousness unless you give* (freely) *of that which you love; and whatever you give, in truth Allah knows it well.* (Sūra Āl 'Imrān, 92)

CHAPTER SEVENTEEN

On Fasting Prescribed by the Religion and On Spiritual Fasting

THE fasting prescribed by the religion is to abstain from eating and drinking and sexual intercourse from dawn to sunset, while spiritual fasting is, in addition, to protect all the senses and thoughts from all that is unlawful. It is to abandon all that is disharmonious, inwardly as well as outwardly. The slightest breach of that intention breaks the fast. Religious fasting is limited by time, while spiritual fasting is forever and lasts throughout one's temporal and eternal life. This is true fasting.

Our Master the Prophet ﷺ says, 'There are many of those who fast who get only hunger and thirst for their efforts and no other benefit'. There are also those who break their fast when they eat, and those whose fast continues even after they have eaten. These are the ones who keep their senses and their thoughts free of evil and their hands and their tongues from hurting others. It is for these that Allah Most High promises, 'Fasting is a deed done for My sake, and I am the one who gives its reward.' About the two kinds of fasting our Master the Prophet ﷺ says, 'The one who fasts has two satisfactions. One is when he breaks his fast at the end of the day. The other is when he sees.'

Those who know the outer form of the religion say that the first satisfaction of the one who fasts is the pleasure of eating after a day of fasting, and the meaning of the satisfaction 'when he sees' is when someone who fasted the whole month of Ramaḍān sees the new moon marking the end of the fast and beginning the festivities of the holiday. The ones who know the inner meaning of fasting say that the joy of breaking the fast is the day when the believer will enter Paradise and partake of the delights therein, and the meaning of the greater joy of seeing is when the faithful sees the truth of Allah with the secret eye of his heart.

Worthier than these two kinds of fasting is the fast of truth, which is in preventing the heart from worshipping any other than the Essence of Allah. It is performed by rendering the eye of the heart blind to all that exists, even in the secret realms outside of this world, except the love of Allah. For although Allah has created all and everything for man, He has created man only for Himself, and He says 'Man is My secret and I am his secret'. That secret is a light from the divine light of Allah. It is the centre of the heart, made out of the finest of matter. It is the soul which knows all the secret truths; it is the secret connection between the created one and his Creator. That secret does not love nor lean towards anything other than Allah.

There is nothing worthy to wish for, there is no other goal, no other beloved in this world and in the hereafter, except Allah. If an atom of anything other than the love of Allah enters the heart, the fast of truth, the true fast, is broken. Then one has to make it up, to revive that wish and intention, to return back to His love, here and in the hereafter. For Allah says: 'Fasting is only for Me, and only I give its reward'.

CHAPTER EIGHTEEN

On the Pilgrimage to Makka and the Inner Pilgrimage to the Essence of the Heart

PILGRIMAGE according to religious precepts is the visitation of the Ka'ba in the city of Makka. There are certain requirements connected with this Pilgrimage: to wear the pilgrim's garb—two wrappers of seamless white cloth which represent the leaving behind of all worldly ties; to arrive in Makka in a state of ablution; to perform seven circumambulations around the Ka'ba—a sign of complete surrender; to run seven times between Ṣafā and Marwa; to go to the plain of 'Arafāt and stand waiting until sunset; to spend the night in Muzdalifa; to make a sacrifice at Mina; to make another seven circumambulations around the Ka'ba; to drink from the well of Zamzam; and to make two cycles of prayer near the place where the prophet Abraham ﷺ stood near the Ka'ba. When these are done, the Pilgrimage is complete and its reward granted, and if anything is lacking in this ritual its reward is cancelled. Allah Most High says: *And complete the pilgrimage and the visitation for Allah.* (Sūra Baqara, 196) When all this is complete, many connections with the world that were unlawful during the ritual become lawful again. In one's normal state one makes a last circumambulation, and returns to daily life. The reward of the pilgrimage is announced by Allah:

> *And whoever enters it is safe, and the Pilgrimage to the House is a duty that men owe to Allah, whoever can find a way to it.* (Sūra Āl 'Imrān, 97)

Whoever can perform the Pilgrimage will find safety from hellfire. That is his reward.

The inner Pilgrimage necessitates a great deal of preparation and gathering of provisions prior to undertaking the voyage. The first thing is to find a guide, a teacher, whom one loves and respects, on whom one depends and whom one obeys. It is he who will furnish the pilgrim with the provisions he needs.

Then one must prepare one's heart. To wake it up one recites the sacred phrase *Lā ilāha illā Llāh*—'there is no god but Allah'—and remembers Allah in contemplating the meaning of that phrase. With this the heart awakens, becomes alive. It also remembers Allah, and keeps remembering Allah until the whole inner being is purified and cleansed of all else but Him.

After the inner purification, one must recite the Names of the attributes of Allah, which will kindle the light of Allah's beauty and grace. It is in that light that one hopes to see the Ka'ba of the secret essence. Allah ordered His prophets Abraham and Ishmael to this purification in saying:

> *Associate not anything with Me, and purify My House for those who circumambulate it.* (Sūra Ḥajj, 26)

Indeed the material Ka'ba in the city of Makka is kept clean for the pilgrims. How much cleaner should one keep the inner Ka'ba upon which Truth will gaze!

After these preparations the inner pilgrim wraps himself in the light of the holy spirit, transforming his material shape into the inner essence, and circumambulates the Ka'ba of the heart, inwardly reciting the second divine Name—ALLĀH, the proper name of God. He moves in circles because the path of the essence is not straight but circular. Its end is its beginning.

Then he goes to the 'Arafāt of the heart, that inner place of supplication, that place where one hopes to know the secret of 'There is no god but He, Who is One and Who has no partners'. There he stands reciting the third Name, HŪ—not alone, but with Him, for Allah *says And He is with you wherever you are.* (Sūra Ḥadīd, 4) Then he recites the fourth Name—ḤAQQ, the Truth, the name of the light of Allah's Essence—and then the fifth Name, ḤAYY—the divine life, eternal, from which all temporal life derives. Then he joins the divine Name of the Ever living with the sixth Name—QAYYŪM, the Self-existing One upon whom all existence depends. This brings him to the Muzdalifa of the centre of the heart.

Then he is brought to the Mina of the sacred secret, the essence, where he recites the seventh Name—QAHHĀR, He Who overwhelms all, the All-compeller. With the power of that Name the self and selfishness are sacrificed. The veils of disbelief are blown away and the gates of the void fly open.

Concerning the veils separating the created from the Creator, the Prophet ﷺ says: 'Faith and faithlessness exist at a place beyond Allah's Throne. They are veils separating the Lord from the view of His servants. One is black and the other white.'

Then the head of the holy spirit is shaved of all the material attributes.

Reciting the eighth divine Name, WAHHĀB—the Donor of All, without limits, without conditions—he enters the sacred area of the Essence. There he recites the ninth Name—FATTĀḤ, the Opener of all that is closed.

Entering the place of assiduousness where he stays in retreat close to Allah, in intimacy with Him and away from everything else, he recites the tenth Name, WĀḤID—Allah the One Who has no equal, none like Him. There he begins to see the manifestation of Allah's attribute ṢAMAD, the Source. He sees the beginning of this inexhaustible treasure. It is a sight without form or shape, resembling nothing.

Then the last circumambulation starts: seven circuits during which he recites the last six Names and adds the eleventh Name, AḤAD—the Unique One, the Only One. Then he drinks from the hand of the intimacy of Allah. *And their Lord makes them drink a pure drink.* (Sūra Insān, 21) The cup in which this drink is offered is the twelfth divine Name, ṢAMAD—the Source, the Satisfier of all needs, the Sole Recourse.

In drinking from this Source one sees all the veils lifting from the eternal face. One looks upon it with the light coming from It. That world has no likeness, no shape, no form. It is indescribable, unassociable, that world 'which no eyes have seen, no ears have heard its description, that no man's heart remembers'. The words of Allah are not heard by sound nor seen as the written word. The delight that no man's heart can taste is the delight in seeing the truth of Allah Most High, and hearing Him speak.

After the Pilgrimage all wrong turns into right. During the Pilgrimage all that is unlawful is transformed into lawful things, and all this is within the now attained unity, which is continuous. Allah says,

> *He who repents and believes and does righteous deeds, for him Allah will change his evil deeds to good.* (Sūra Furqān, 70)

Then that pilgrim will be freed of all actions that are from himself and freed from all fear and grief. Allah says: *Now surely the friends of Allah, they have no fear, nor do they grieve.* (Sūra Yūnus, 62) Finally the farewell circumambulation is performed with the recitation of all the divine Names.

Then the pilgrim returns home, to the home of his origin, that holy land where Allah created man in the best and most beautiful pattern. In returning he recites the twelfth divine Name, ṢAMAD, the Source, the treasure from which the needs of all creation are satisfied. That is the world of Allah's proximity, that is where the home of the inner pilgrim is, and that is where he returns.

This is all that can be explained, as much as the tongue can say and the mind grasp. Beyond this no news can be given, for beyond is the unperceivable, inconceivable, indescribable. As the Prophet ﷺ says, 'There is a knowledge that stays intact like buried treasure. None can know it and none can find it except those who are given the divine knowledge.' But when they hear of the existence of such knowledge, the sincere do not deny it.

The man of ordinary knowledge gathers what he gathers from the surface. The one who possesses divine wisdom draws from the depths. The wisdom of the wise is the very secret of Allah Most

High. None knows what He knows other than He himself. Allah says:

And they encompass nothing of His knowledge except what He pleases. His knowledge extends over the heavens and the earth and the preservation of both tire Him not. (Sūra Baqara, 255)

Those blessed ones with whom He shares His knowledge are His prophets and His beloved ones who strive to come close to Him.

He knows the secret and what is yet more hidden. (Sūra Ṭā Hā, 7)

Allah, there is no god but He, His are the Most Beautiful Names. (Sūra Ṭā Hā, 8)

And Allah knows best.

CHAPTER NINETEEN

On Witnessing Divine Truth through the State of Peace Coming from Abandonment of the Worldly and through Ecstasy

MANY verses in the Qur'ān and many declarations of the Prophet ﷺ and the saints describe these states. To cite a few: Allah says in His Qur'ān,

> *The bodies of those who* [love and] *fear their Lord tremble, then their bodies soften as their hearts remember Allah. This is Allah's guidance, He guides therewith whom He pleases.* (Sūra Zumar, 23)

and

> *Is one whose heart Allah has opened to the submission of Islam, so that he follows a light from his Lord* (no better than one hard-hearted)? *Woe to those whose hearts are hardened against the remembrance of Allah.* (Sūra Zumar, 22)

The Prophet ﷺ says, 'A single divine inspiration which cuts one off from the world and bestows upon one the reflection of divine attributes, showing one the signs of the divine Unity, is worth the experience of both worlds.' And 'The one who has not experienced ecstasy and thereby received the manifestation of divine wisdom and truth has not lived.'

Ḥaḍrat Junayd, may Allah be pleased with him, said, 'When ecstasy meets the divine manifestations inside one, one is either in a state of the highest joy or the deepest sorrow.'

There are two kinds of ecstasy: physical ecstasy and spiritual ecstasy. Physical ecstasy is a product of the ego. It does not give one any spiritual satisfaction. It is under the influence of the senses. Often it is hypocritical, occurring so that others see or hear about it. This kind of ecstasy is totally devoid of value because it is purposeful, it is willed: the one who experiences it still thinks that he can do, that he can choose. It is not good to give any importance to such experiences.

Spiritual ecstasy, however, is a totally different state, a state caused by the overflow of spiritual energy. Ordinarily, exterior influences—such as a beautifully recited poem, or the Qur'ān chanted by a beautiful voice, or the excitement brought on by the ceremony of remembrance of the Sufis—may cause this spiritual elevation. This happens because at such moments the physical resistance of the being is obliterated. The will, the ability of the mind to choose and to decide, is overcome. When the powers of both the body and the mind are undermined, the ecstatic state is purely spiritual. To go along with that kind of experience is beneficial to one.

Allah Most High says:

> *So give the good news to My servants who listen to the word* (of Allah), *then follow the beauty in it. Such are they whom Allah has guided. And such are the men of understanding.* (Sūra Zumar, 17–18)

The sweet singing of the birds, the sighing of lovers, are among those exterior causes which move the spiritual energy. In this state of spiritual energy evil and the ego have no share; the Devil operates within the dark realms of the doings of the ego and has no say in the illuminated realm of mercy. In the realm of Allah's mercy and compassion evil melts like salt in water, just as it evaporates when one recites with faith the divine phrase *Lā ḥawla walā quwwata illā bi-Llāh il-'Alī il-'Aẓīm*—'There is neither force nor power except in Allah the Glorious and Exalted'. The influences which incite spiritual ecstasy are described in the words of the Prophet ﷺ, 'The verses of the Qur'ān, the wise and wondrous poems of love and sounds and voices of yearning illuminate the face of the soul'.

True ecstasy is the conjunction of light with light, when the soul of man meets the divine light. Allah says, *The pure are for the pure.* (Sūra Nūr, 26) If ecstasy comes through the influence of the ego and of the Devil, there is no light there. There is only disbelief, doubt, denial and confusion. Darkness begets darkness. That is the ego's portion. In that portion the soul and the spirit have no share. Allah says, *The impure are for the impure* (Sūra Nūr, 26)

The manifestation of the state of ecstasy is also of two kinds—the manifestation of physical ecstasy is subject to one's own will while the manifestation of spiritual ecstasy is beyond one's choice and volition; in the first case the apparent signs are voluntary. If one shakes and trembles and moans even though not under the influence of any pain or disturbance in the body, it is not considered legitimate. What is legitimate is visible changes in one's physical condition that are involuntary and caused by one's inner state.

These involuntary manifestations are the result of a spiritual force over which one has no control. The soul in ecstasy overwhelms the senses. It is like the state of delirium caused by a high fever: it is hardly possible to prevent oneself from shaking and trembling and stiffening in delirium because one has no power over any of these exterior manifestations. Similarly when expanded spiritual energy overcomes the will of the mind and the body, ecstasy is true, sincere and spiritual.

Such spiritual ecstatic states, which the intimates of Allah enter in performing the movements and whirling of their rituals, are means to excite and impel their hearts. This is the food of those who love Allah: it gives them energy in their hard voyage in search of the truth. Our Master the Prophet ﷺ says, 'The ecstatic ritual of the lovers of Allah, their whirling and chanting, is an obligatory form of worship for some, and for others a supererogatory act of worship—and yet for others still it is heresy. It is obligatory for the perfect man, it is supererogatory for the lovers and for the heedless it is heresy.' And 'He is ill-natured who takes no pleasure being with lovers of Allah: the poems of the wise which they chant, the season of spring, the colour and perfume of its flowers and the lute and its song.'

The heedless for whom the seeking of spiritual ecstasy is a heresy, and the ill-natured ones who take no pleasure in beauty, are sick and there is no remedy for that sickness. They are lower than the birds and the beasts, lower even than the ass, because even the animal takes pleasure in a tune. When the Prophet David (peace be upon him) sang, all the birds gathered around him to listen to his beautiful voice. The Prophet ﷺ says, 'The one who has not experienced ecstasy does not have the taste of his religion'.

There are ten states of ecstasy. Some of these are apparent and their signs visible, and some are hidden and unobservable by others, like the inner consciousness and remembrance of Allah, or a silent reading of the Holy Qur'ān. To shed tears, to have deep feelings of regret, fear of Allah's punishment, longing and sorrow, shame for one's moments of unconsciousness; when one grows pale, or the face flushes with excitement from states within and from events around one, burning with the yearning for Allah—these and all physical and spiritual anomalies caused by such things are signs of ecstasy.

CHAPTER TWENTY

On Withdrawing from the World into Seclusion and On Solitude

SECLUSION and solitude should be viewed as states of both exterior and interior withdrawal.

The exterior state of seclusion is when a man decides to withdraw himself from the world, imprisoning himself in a space away from other people, so that people in the world are saved from his undesirable character and existence. He also hopes that in so doing the source of his undesirable existence, his ego and the base desires of his flesh, will be separated from their daily nourishment and the satisfaction of things they are used to. Further, he hopes that this isolation will educate his ego and his appetites, permitting the development of his inner spiritual being.

When one decides this, one's intention must be sincere. In a way it is like wilfully putting oneself in a grave, in a state of death, hoping above all for the agreement and pleasure of Allah, wishing in one's heart to rid the pure and the faithful of one's ugly presence. The Prophet ﷺ says, 'The faithful is he from whose hand and tongue the other faithful are safe'.

Indeed, he locks his tongue from idle talk, for as the Prophet says, 'The salvation of man comes from his tongue. His villainy and disgrace come also from his tongue'. He shuts his eyes to the unlawful so that their treacherous, deceitful sight does not fall on what belongs to others. He stops his ears from hearing lies and evil, and ties his feet, preventing them from carrying him to sin.

Our Master the Prophet ﷺ points out that members of the body can sin by themselves: 'The eyes can commit adultery'. When one of your senses or one of your members sins, an ugly black creature is created out of it on the day of the Last Judgment and it witnesses against you for the sin it committed. Then it is cast into hellfire.'

God praises the one who prevents himself from wrongdoing, because this is true penitence, active repentance. He says,

> *And as for he who fears to stand before his Lord and who restrains himself from base desires, the Garden is surely the abode.* (Sūra Nāzi'āt, 40–41)

He who fears his Lord and repents, withdrawing his ugly existence from among the faithful and withdrawing his ugliness from his own faithfulness, is transformed in his isolation into a beautiful young man. He becomes the servant of the inhabitants of Paradise.

Seclusion is a castle against the enemy of one's own sins and errors. Within it, alone, one is kept clean. God says,

> *So whoever hopes to meet his Lord, he should do good deeds and join no one in the service of his Lord.* (Sūra Kahf, 110)

All that has been told up to now is only the outer meaning of the state of seclusion. The inner meaning of seclusion is the exclusion from the heart of even the thought of anything that belongs in the realm of the worldly, of evil and of the ego, leaving food and drink and belongings, family, wife, children and the care and love of all.

The thought of others seeing or hearing must not enter that seclusion. The Prophet ﷺ says, 'Fame and that which it brings is a calamity, and to turn away from fame and seeking approval from others and that which they bring is a comfort.' He who intends to enter into inner seclusion has to lock out of his heart all pride, arrogance, vengeance, tyranny, anger, envy, intolerance, slander and their like. If any such feeling enters the one in seclusion, his heart becomes soiled. It is no longer withdrawn from the world, and such seclusion is worthless. Once dirt enters the heart it loses its purity and all good is cancelled. God says,

> *What you have brought is deception. Surely God makes all your works come to nothing.* (Sūra Yūnus, 81)

Even if one's actions appear good to other people, when negative characteristics enter into them one is considered a mischief maker who deceives himself and others. The Prophet ﷺ says: 'Pride and arrogance corrupt faith. Slander and backbiting are worse sins than adultery'; 'As fire burns firewood, vengeance burns and consumes all one's good deeds.' 'Intrigue sleeps; a curse be upon the one who wakes it up.' 'The miser will never enter Paradise, even if he spend his whole life praying.' 'Hypocrisy is a hidden form of setting up others and oneself as partners to Allah.' 'Paradise will reject the one who rejects others.'

There are many more signs of bad character condemned by the Messenger of Allah. Those mentioned suffice to show us that this world is a place which requires constant prudence and precaution, that one has to walk through it with extreme care and attention. The first goal of the mystic path is the cleansing of the heart, and the first action necessary to achieve this is to deny the ego and the flesh their futile and vain desires. In seclusion, with silence, meditation and continuous remembrance, one's ego is reformed. Then Allah Most High renders one's heart enlightened.

Nothing that happens in seclusion should be done wilfully and purposefully. That which is necessary is love, sincerity and true faith. The way is not one's own way. One is following the way of the blessed Companions of the Prophet, the way of those who followed them, and the way of those who know their way and who follow it.

When the faithful one in this way follows the path of repentance and inspiration and cleanses his heart, Allah Most High withdraws from him all that is harmful and evil and keeps him secure from their returning. His appearance becomes beautiful; his feelings, whether contained or expressed, become pure. All that he does is done in reverence, for he is in the divine presence. 'Allah hears the one who gives grateful praise.' Thus Allah watches over him. Allah accepts his prayers and his yearnings and his grateful praise and grants him all he wishes. Allah says,

> *If any do seek glory and power—to Allah belong all glory and power. To Him ascend* (all) *words of purity. It is He Who exalts each deed of righteousness. . .* (Sūra Fāṭir, 10)

Words of purity safeguard the tongue from heedless words. The tongue is a beautiful instrument to praise the Lord, to repeat His Beautiful Names, to confirm His Unity. Allah warns against heedless talk.

> *Secure indeed are the believers who are humble in their prayers and who shun vain talk.* (Sūra Mu'minūn, 1–3)

Allah Most High bestows His mercy, compassion, and grace upon the one who learns and acts with good intention. He brings him close by raising his level. He is pleased with him; He forgives his faults.

When one is lifted to that level, one's heart becomes like an ocean. The shape and colour of that ocean do not change with the little cruelty and torment that men drop into it. The blessed Prophet ﷺ says, 'Be like an ocean whose appearance does not change, but in which the dark soldiers of your ego drown'—as the Pharaoh and his armies drowned in the Red Sea. On that ocean, the ship of religion floats safe and sound; it sails upon that great ocean. The spirit of the one in seclusion dives into its depths to find the pearl of truth, brings to the surface pearls of wisdom and coral of grace, and spreads them abroad. Allah says, *Out of them come pearls and coral.* (Sūra Raḥmān, 22)

To contain such an ocean, your appearance must be the same as your being; what you are must be the same as what you appear to be. Your exterior and interior states must be one. When this happens, there is no duplicity, sedition or disorder in the ocean of the heart. No storm of mischief can brew in that calm sea. The one who attains that state is in a state of complete repentance; his knowledge is vast and beneficent, his acts are all service to others, his heart does not flow to evil. If he errs or forgets, he is forgiven, for he remembers when he forgets and repents when he errs. He is in the proximity of his Lord and of himself.

CHAPTER TWENTY-ONE

Prayers and Recitations Pertaining to the Path of Seclusion

WHOSOEVER has chosen to withdraw himself from the world in order to come close to God must know the appropriate prayers and recitations. Performing these prayers requires that one be in a state of purity and as much as possible in a state of fasting. The space within which the secluded one closes himself is usually in or in the near vicinity of a mosque, for it is a condition of seclusion to leave one's cell five times a day to perform congregational prayers, all the while remaining impersonal and hidden and not speaking a word. Whoever is in seclusion must make a special effort to be more conscious of and abide with the principles, fundamentals and conditions of congregational prayer.

Every night in the middle of the night the secluded person must wake up to perform the prayer called *tahajjud*, meaning the state of wakefulness in the middle of sleep. The *tahajjud* prayer bears the symbolism of resurrection after death. When one wakes up for this prayer one is the owner of one's heart and one's thoughts are clear. In order not to spoil this conscious state one should not then participate in ordinary activities of life such as eating and drinking.

Immediately on awakening, with the realization of resurrected consciousness, recite: *al-ḥamdu li-'Llāhi 'lladhī aḥyānī baʿda mā amātanī wa-ilayhin-nushūr*—'All praise to Allah Who has resurrected me after having taken my life. After death, all will revive and go to Him'. Then recite the last ten verses of the Sūra Āl ʿImrān:

Behold! In the creation of the heavens and the earth, and the alternation of night and day there are indeed signs for men of understanding—

Men who celebrate the praises of God standing, sitting, and lying down on their sides, and contemplate the (wonders of) *creation in the heavens and the earth* (with the thought): *'Our Lord! Not for naught hast Thou created* (all) *this! Glory to Thee! Give us salvation from the penalty of the Fire.'*

Our Lord! any whom Thou dost admit to the Fire, truly Thou coverest with shame, and never will wrongdoers find any helpers!

Our Lord! we have heard the call of one calling (us) *to faith, 'Believe ye in the Lord', and we have believed. Our Lord! Forgive us our sins, blot out from us our iniquities, and take to Thyself our souls in the company of the righteous.*

Our Lord! Grant us what Thou didst promise unto us through Thine Apostles, and save us from shame on the Day of Judgment, for Thou never breakest Thy promise.

And their Lord hath accepted of them, and answered them: 'Never will I suffer to be lost the work of any of you, be he male or female: Ye are members, one of another: Those who have left their homes, or been driven out there from, or suffered harm in My cause, or fought or been slain—verily I will blot out from them their iniquities and admit them into Gardens with rivers flowing beneath;—a reward from the Presence of Allah, and from His Presence is the best of rewards.'

Let not the strutting about of the unbelievers through the land deceive thee.

Little is it for enjoyment: Their ultimate abode is Hell: what an evil bed (to lie on)*!*

On the other hand, for those who fear their Lord, are Gardens with rivers flowing beneath; therein are they to dwell (for ever)—*a gift from the Presence of Allah; and that which is in the Presence of Allah is the best* (bliss) *for the righteous.*

And there are, certainly, among the People of the Book (the Christians and Jews) *those who believe in Allah, in the revelation to you, and in the revelation to them, bowing in humility to Allah: They will not sell the signs of Allah for a miserable gain! For them is a reward with their Lord, and Allah is swift in account.*

O ye who believe! Persevere in patience and constancy; vie in such perseverance; strengthen each other; and fear Allah; that ye may prosper. (Sūra Āl ʿImrān, 190–200)

Following this one takes ablution and prays: 'Glory to Allah—all praise is due to You. None other than You is worthy to receive prayer. I repent for my sins. Forgive my sins, forgive my very existence. Accept my repentance. You are the Merciful, You like to forgive. O Lord, place me among those who realize their wrongdoings and include me among Your pure servants who have patience, who are thankful, who remember You and who praise You night and day.'

Then raising one's eyes to the night sky one confirms, 'I witness that there is no god but Allah, alone, without a partner, and I witness that Muḥammad is Allah's servant and His Messenger.'

'I take refuge in Your mercy from Your punishment. I take refuge in Your pleasure and approval from Your wrath. I take refuge in You from You. I cannot know You as You know Yourself. I cannot praise You enough. I am Your servant, I am the son of Your servant. My forehead, upon which You have written my destiny, is in Your hand. Your decree runs through me. What You have ordained for me is right for me. I set before You my hands and the bounties You have placed in them. I open myself in front of You, exposing all of my sins. There is no god but You, and You are merciful and I am a tyrant. I am a doer of wrong, I have tyrannized myself. For my sake, because I am Your servant, forgive my great sins. You are my Lord, You are the only one who can forgive.'

Then turning in the direction of the *qibla*, say: 'Allah is the most great. All praise is due to Him. I remember and glorify Him night and day'. Then repeat ten times: 'All glory is to Allah', then ten times: 'All praise and thanks are to Allah', then ten times: 'There is no god but Allah'.

Next one performs twelve cycles of prayer. One gives the closing greeting of peace after every two cycles, because our Master the Prophet ﷺ said, 'The night prayers are done two by two'.

Allah Most High praises those who offer the prayer of wakefulness:

> *And during a part of the night keep awake and pray beyond what is incumbent upon you. Maybe your Lord will raise you to a state of great glory.* (Sūra Banī Isrā'īl, 79)

> *They forsake their beds, calling on their Lord in fear and in hope, and spend out of what We have given them. So no soul knows what refreshment of the eyes is hidden for them, a reward for what they did.* (Sūra Sajda, 16–17)

Later in the night, one wakes up again to perform the three cycles of *witr* prayer that seal the prayers of the day. In the third cycle, after reciting the Fātiḥa— the Opening:

In the name of Allah, the Beneficent, the Merciful
Praise be to Allah, the Lord of the worlds,
The Beneficent, the Merciful,
Master of the Day of Judgment
You do we serve and You do we beseech for help
Guide us on the straight path
The path of those upon whom You have bestowed favours
Not of those upon whom wrath is brought down nor of those who go astray.

and one other chapter from the Qur'ān, one raises one's hands as at the beginning of the prayer, says *Allāhu akbar*—'Allah is most great'—and recites the *qunūt*, the prayer of reverence: 'O Allah, we ask Your help and we ask Your forgiveness and Your guidance. We are faithful to You and we turn to You and we trust in You and we praise You for all good. We are thankful to You and we are not ungrateful to You, and we renounce and abandon the one who offends You with sins. O Allah, You we serve and to You we pray and prostrate ourselves and to You we have recourse. We hope for Your mercy and fear Your punishment. Surely Your punishment will overtake those who disbelieve.'

The prayer is then finished in the usual way.

After sunrise the one in seclusion performs the *ishrāq* prayer, the prayer of illumination, which is of two cycles, and afterwards two cycles of the *isti'ādha* prayer that seeks refuge and protection from evil. During the first cycle, after the Fātiḥa, one recites the Sūra Falaq, the Dawn:

Say: I seek refuge with the Lord of the Dawn
From the mischief of created things
From the mischief of Darkness as it overspreads from the mischief of those who practice secret arts
And from the mischief of the envious one as he practises envy.

In the second cycle, after the Fātiḥa, one recites the Sūra Nās, Mankind:

Say: I seek refuge with the Lord and Cherisher of Mankind
The King (or Ruler) *of Mankind,*
The God (or judge) *of Mankind—*
From the mischief of the Whisperer (of evil) *who withdraws* (after his whisper)—
(The same) *who whispers into the hearts of mankind—Among jinns and among men.*

Preparing oneself for the day, one next prays two cycles of *istikhāra*, prayer seeking Allah's guidance for right decisions during the day. In each of the two cycles of *istikhāra* the Fātiḥa is followed by the Throne Verse, *āyat al-kursī*:

> *Allah! There is no god but He—the Living, the Self-subsisting, Eternal. No slumber can seize Him nor sleep. His are all things in the heavens and on earth. Who is there who can intercede in His presence except as He permitteth? He knoweth what* (appeareth to His creatures as) *before or behind them. Nor shall they compass aught of his knowledge except as He willeth. His Throne doth extend over the heavens and the earth, and He feeleth no fatigue in guarding and preserving them, for He is the Most High, the Supreme* (in glory).

Then one recites seven times the Sūra Ikhlāṣ, Sincerity:

> *Say: He is God, the One and Only*
> *God the Eternal, Absolute*
> *He begetteth not, nor is He begotten*
> *And there in none like unto Him.*

Later in the morning, the one in seclusion performs the *Ḍuḥā* prayer of piety and peace of heart. It is performed in six cycles, with a recitation of verses from the Sūra Shams, the Sun, and the Sūra Ḍuḥā, the Brightness of Day:

> *By the sun and his* (glorious) *splendour;*
> *By the moon as she follows him;*
> *By the day as it shows up* (the sun's) *glory;*
> *By the night as it conceals it;*
> *By the firmament and its* (wonderful) *structure;*
> *By the earth and its* (wide) *expanse;*
> *By the soul and the proportion and order given to it;*
> *And its enlightenment as to its wrong and its right;—*
> *Truly he succeeds that purifies it,*
> *And he fails that corrupts it!*
> *The Thamud* (people) *rejected* (their prophet) *through their inordinate wrongdoing.*

Behold, the most wicked man among them was deputed (for impiety).
But the Apostle of Allah said to them: 'It is a she-camel of Allah! And (bar her not from) *having her drink!'*
Then they rejected him (as a false prophet), *and they hamstrung her. So their Lord, on account of their crime, obliterated their traces and made them equal* (in destruction, high and low!)
And for Him is no fear of its consequences.

* * *

By the glorious morning light,
And by the night when it is still—
Thy Guardian—Lord hath not forsaken thee, nor is He displeased.
And verily the hereafter will be better for thee than the present,
And soon will thy Guardian-Lord give thee (that wherewith) *thou shalt be well-pleased.*
Did He not find thee an orphan and give thee shelter (and care)*?*
And He found thee wandering, and He gave thee guidance.
And He found thee in need, and made thee independent.
Therefore treat not the orphan with harshness,
Nor repulse the petitioner (unheard);
But the bounty of thy Lord—rehearse and proclaim!

The *ḍuḥā* prayer is followed by two cycles of *kaffāra*, a prayer of expiation for dirt that may have touched one unavoidably or without one's being aware. For contact with filth, even when inadvertent, is nonetheless a sin, a cause of punishment. This may happen even in seclusion, for instance, through one's physiological needs. The Prophet ﷺ says, 'Beware of dirt—even when you urinate, that a drop should not splash on you—because it is a sign of the suffering of the grave.' In each cycle, after the Fātiḥa one repeats the Sūra Kawthar seven times:

In the name of Allah the Beneficent and Merciful.
To you have We granted the fountain (of abundance),
Therefore to your Lord turn in prayer and sacrifice.
For he who hates you, he will be cut off (from future hope).

Another prayer—long, though it is only four cycles—should be performed in the course of a day in seclusion. This is the *tasbīḥ*, glorification, prayer. If the believer belongs to the Ḥanafī school he will give the greeting of peace and finish only after all four cycles; if he is of the Shāfi'ī school he will offer it as two sets of two cycles. (This rule applies to prayer done during the day. If it is done at night, both the Ḥanafiyya and the Shāfi'iyya perform the prayer in two sets of two cycles.)

The Prophet ﷺ described this prayer to his uncle, Ibn 'Abbās, thus:

'O 'Abbās, my beloved uncle, be heedful, I will give you a gift. Be heedful, I am going to transmit to you something good; be heedful, I am going to give you new life and hope; be heedful, I am going to give you something worth ten of the greatest goods. If you do what I tell you, Allah will forgive your sins—those you committed before and those you will commit after, old ones, new ones, small ones, large ones, made knowingly or unknowingly, secretly or openly.

'You will perform four cycles of prayer. In each cycle, after the Fātiḥa, you will recite another chapter from the Qur'ān. While you are standing, you will repeat fifteen times: *Subḥāna Llāhi, il-ḥamdu li-Llāhi, lā ilāha illā Llāhu wa-Llāhu akbar, wa-lā ḥawla wa-lā quwwata illā bi-Llāhi l-'Alī l-'Aẓīm*—"Glory to Allah, all praise belongs to Allah, there is no god but Allah, and Allah is Most Great. There is no power or strength except in Allah, the Exalted, the Magnificent".'

'When you bow from the waist, hands on knees, you will repeat this ten more times. Then stand and repeat it ten more times; then prostrate and repeat it ten more times. Rising from the prostration, sitting upon your knees, repeat it ten more times. Prostrate yourself again and repeat it ten more times. Sit again on your knees and repeat it ten more times, then stand for the second cycle. Do the same during the rest of the four cycles.

'If you can, do this prayer every day. If you cannot, do it every Friday. If you cannot, do it every month. If you cannot, do it once a year; if you cannot do this either, do it at least once in your lifetime.'

Thus in the four cycles. The prayer of praise is repeated three hundred times. As the Prophet ﷺ suggested the exercise of this prayer to his uncle, Ibn 'Abbās, may Allah be pleased with him, it is suggested that the one in seclusion also perform it.

In addition to these duties the secluded person should read at least two hundred verses from the Holy Qur'ān each day.

He should also remember Allah continuously and, according to his inner state, either proclaim His Beautiful Names aloud or inwardly in his heart. The inner silent remembrance begins only when the heart regains consciousness and life. The language of this remembrance is the hidden secret word.

Everyone remembers Allah and recites His Names in accordance with his own ability. Allah says: *And remember Him in the way He has guided you.* (Sūra Baqara, 198) In other words, remember Him according to your ability. At every spiritual level the remembrance is different. It has another name; it has another character, another way. Only the ones who are at each level know its proper remembrance.

The one in seclusion also recites the chapter of Sincerity and Unity, the Sūra Ikhlāṣ, a hundred times every day.

He also prays for our Master the Prophet ﷺ, reciting one hundred times: *Allāhumma ṣalli 'alā Sayyidinā Muḥammādin wa-'alā āli Muḥammādin wa-ṣaḥbihi wa-sallim*—'O God, pour blessings upon our Master Muḥammad and upon the family of Muḥammad and his Companions, and peace.'

He should also recite the following prayer one hundred times:

> *astaghfiru Llāh al-'Aẓīm lā ilāha illā Huwa l-Ḥayy ul-Qayyūm—mimā qaddamtu wa-mā akhkhartu wa-mā 'alantu wa-ma asrartu wa-mā asraftu wa-mā anta a 'lamu bihi minnī. Anta l-Muqaddimu wa-antal-Mu'akhkhiru wa-anta 'alā kulli shay 'in Qadīr*

'I beg forgiveness from Allah the Everliving, the Self-Existing, the Magnificent—there is no god but He. I ask forgiveness for my sins of the past and of the future, the wrongs I have done openly and secretly, and for my life which I have squandered. You know me better than I do myself. You bring things forth and leave them behind, and You have power over everything.'

The time left after all of this is completed is spent reading from the Qur'ān and in further worship and prayer.

CHAPTER TWENTY-TWO

On Dreams

THE dreams that are dreamt between the time just before one falls asleep and deep sleep are true and beneficent. These dreams are often bearers of revelations and the medium of miracles. They are the images that fall on the eye of the heart. The proof of the truth of dreams is in the words of Allah:

> *Allah indeed fulfilled the dream of his messenger with truth: you shall certainly enter the sacred mosque, if Allah please, in security.* (Sūra Fatḥ, 27)

And indeed the Prophet ﷺ did enter the holy mosque in Makka, which was held by his enemies, the year after this dream. Another example is in the dream of the prophet Joseph (peace be upon him):

> *When Joseph said to his father, O my father, I dreamt of eleven stars and the sun and the moon, I saw them making obeisance to me.* (Sūra Yūsuf, 4)

The Prophet ﷺ said, 'No other prophets will come after me, yet there may come other revelations. The believers will see these revelations in their dreams, or the revelations will be shown to them in their dreams.' Allah confirms this:

> *For them is the revelation of good news in the life of this world and in the hereafter.* (Sūra Yūnus, 64)

Dreams come from Allah, but sometimes also from the accursed Devil.

The Prophet ﷺ says, 'The one who sees me in his dreams certainly sees me, because the Devil cannot take my shape.' Neither can the Devil appear in the form of those who follow the faith, the path, the wisdom, the truth and the light of the Prophet ﷺ. The ones who know interpret these words of the Prophet ﷺ, saying that not only can the Devil not take the form of the Prophet ﷺ, he cannot pretend to be anyone or anything which has the character of mercy and beneficence, or compassion and grace and faith. Indeed, all the prophets and the saints and the angels, the holy mosque of the Ka'ba, the sun, the moon, the white clouds, the Holy Qur'ān, are entities into which the Devil cannot enter, nor can he take their shape. This is because the Devil is the place and condition of the manifestation of wrath and punishment and grief. He can only represent confusion and doubt. When someone has in him the manifestation of Allah's Name, the 'Ultimate Guide to Truth', how could the attribute of the One Who Leads Astray be manifest in him? Attributes which are in opposition to each other can never take each other's place, like water and fire. Wrath cannot assume the shape of mercy, neither can fire appear as water. They repel each other, they stay away from each other, they belong to different spaces. Thus Allah separates truth from falsehood. *Thus does Allah manifest truth and falsehood... with parables and examples.* (Sura Ra'd, 17)

On the other hand, the Devil can pretend to be Allah and tempt people, leading them astray. This he can do only with the permission of Allah. Allah has many attributes which appear to be contrary to each other. For instance, His attribute of might and anger appears to be the opposite of his attribute of beauty and gentleness. The accursed Devil can only pretend to assume the character of anger and might because he is in essence the object of Allah's wrath. Allah also has both the attributes of the Ultimate Guide to Truth and the One Who Leads Astray. The Devil cannot appear with the character of any divine attribute in which there is a trace of guidance.

If the Devil pretends to represent any of the attributes of Allah, he does this through Allah's will, in order to lead the believer to good by opposing bad, to lead him to truth by opposing falsehood. In reality the Devil does not have the power to take away the faith of the faithful; he can only pick it up if the believer himself throws it away.

Allah asks his Prophet to:

> *Say: This is my way. I call to Allah with the knowledge of certainty* (obtained by insight), *I and the ones who follow me, and glory be to Allah; and I am not of the ones who attribute partners to Him.* (Sūra Yūsuf, 108)

In this verse, 'the ones who follow me' are the perfect men, the true spiritual teachers who will come after the Prophet ﷺ, who will have his inner knowledge and insight and who will be close to Allah. Such a person is described as *protector and true guide.* (Sūra Kahf,17)

There are two kinds of dreams, subjective and objective, and each is itself divided into two kinds.

The first kind of subjective dream is the reflection of a high spiritual state and a resulting virtue, and appears in images such as the sun, the moon, the stars, white desert scenes bathed in light, gardens of Paradise, palaces, beautiful spirits in angelic form and so on. These are the attributes of a pure heart. The second kind of subjective dream contains images that correspond to the state of the one who is free from anxiety and who has come to know himself and found peace of mind. These images are the delights which he will find in Paradise—the taste of heavenly nourishment, the perfume and sounds of Paradise.

He will dream of some animals and birds that resemble the most beautiful of their counterparts in this world. The animals seen in such dreams are indeed from Paradise. For instance, the camel is an animal of Paradise. The horse is sent as an animal of burden to carry the holy warrior in his battle with the non believer around him and within him. The ox was sent to the prophet Adam عليه السلام to till the ground to grow wheat. The lamb comes from the honey of Paradise, the camel is created from the light of Paradise, the horse from the sweet basil of Paradise, the ox from the saffron of Paradise.

The mule represents the lowest state of the one who has found peace of heart and mind. When he dreams of a mule, it is a sign that he is negligent and lazy in his worship because the desires of his flesh and ego prevent him, and his spiritual efforts are without benefit. Then he should repent and be constant in his good deeds so that he will obtain a result.

The ass was created from the stone of Paradise and is given to the service of Adam عليه السلام and his progeny. The ass is the symbol of the flesh and its material needs, the ego and its selfishness. The flesh is an animal of burden to carry the soul. If man is a slave to his flesh, he is like a man carrying an ass on his shoulders, but the true man rides the ass of his material being. Thus the ass represents the means by which he directs the affairs of the hereafter in this world.

To speak with a beautiful youth with a pure and spiritual countenance is a sign that divine manifestations are reaching one, because those who have reached the enlightenment of divine manifestations in Paradise will appear in this beautiful form. Our Master the Prophet ﷺ describes them as being well-proportioned, graceful with beautiful dark eyes. He even said, 'I have seen my Lord in the shape of a most beautiful youth'. As Allah is beyond all shape and form, this statement is interpreted as the manifestation of the Lord's beautiful attributes reflected upon the mirror of the pure soul. This reflection is called the child of the heart. The material appearance, the body, is the mirror for the divine intelligence which educates and forms us. This reflected image is also the connection between the servant and his Lord. Ḥaḍrat 'Alī, may Allah be pleased with him, said, 'If I were not formed by my Lord I would not have come to know Him'.

For spiritual formation one needs the instruction and example of a guide in the form of a living teacher. These teachers are the prophets and the ones close to Allah who inherit their wisdom. It is Only through their teaching that the heart and the being are illuminated, shedding light on their path. One finds the inspired soul in oneself through them. Allah says:

> *He is the Raiser of levels, the Lord of the Throne of Power. By His order does He send the* (inspired) *soul to any of his servants He pleases, that he may warn* (men) *of the day of meeting* (their Lord). (Sūra Mu'min, 15)

For the salvation of your heart you must find a teacher who will inspire you with this soul.

Imam Ghazālī, may Allah sanctify his secret, says, 'It is lawful to see Allah Most High in one's dreams as a beautiful image. That image is a symbol in accordance with one's spiritual level. That which is seen is certainly not the divine Essence, because Allah is beyond all shape and form. Neither can our Master the Prophet ﷺ be seen in dreams in his true appearance, except by those who are the inheritors of his wisdom, knowledge and actions and who follow him totally. Others, when they dream of him, dream of symbols in accordance with their potential and state, but they do not truly see him.'

In the commentary of Muslim's collection of traditions of the Prophet ﷺ there is a statement which says, 'It is lawful to dream of Allah Most High either as light or in human form'. He manifests Himself in the forms of His attributes. To the Prophet Moses عليه السلام He appeared as fire in a burning jujube tree. That was the apparition of the divine Word which the Prophet Moses heard as the Burning Bush, saying *O Moses, what is that in thy right hand?* (Sūra Ṭā Ḥā, 17)

What appeared to Moses as fire in reality was the divine light. He saw it as fire in accordance with his level and his wish, for he was seeking fire. For man the lowest degree of being is that of vegetation, the tree, and then the level of animal in him. Is there any wonder if the one who has purified himself of these lower levels of being and become a perfect man sees the divine truth manifested as a burning bush? To other perfect men Allah manifested His words as their own, issuing from their own lips. Ḥaḍrat Bāyazīd al-Bisṭāmī, may Allah sanctify his secret, in such a state of divine inspiration pronounced the words, 'My essence is the Glorious One. How great is my honour!' The divine word came from the lips of Ḥaḍrat Junayd al-Baghdādī, may Allah be pleased with him, 'There is none other than Allah under my cloak.' There are great secrets in levels such as these which perfect men have reached. They are too difficult to comprehend and too long to explain here. They concern only those who dedicate their lives to the pursuit of inner knowledge.

To be a recipient of divine manifestation and to have contact with the spirit of our Master the Prophet ﷺ one must be taught and educated and brought to a certain spiritual level. The seeker who has just entered the spiritual path cannot hope to be able to relate to Allah Most High or to His Prophet ﷺ without an intermediary. He must first be prepared and educated by a teacher who is close to them. Between a pure teacher who is close to Allah and our Master the Prophet ﷺ there is a relationship which transcends the physical. If the Prophet ﷺ were alive one could take knowledge directly from him and there would be no need of an intermediary. But as he has passed to the hereafter, he is separated from the worldly and in an immaterial state. Therefore one cannot have direct contact with him. The same is true of the true teachers. When they leave this world one can no longer learn from them.

You will understand if you are perceptive; if you are not, seek to be. Seek to find this understanding with contemplation so that you will overcome the darkness of the ego with the light of illumination. You need light to see, to understand: you cannot see in the dark. The light falls only on places that have been put in order and cleansed, on honoured places. The beginner by himself cannot put himself in order and therefore is in need of a teacher.

A living teacher must have connection with our Master the Prophet of Allah ﷺ—that is, if he is truly the inheritor of the state of the Prophet. In his teaching he receives guidance from the Prophet and is taught to be a true servant of Allah. With this help he becomes the means of continuation of the inner path. The rest is a secret. Only the ones fit to realize may realize.

> *The might*, (the true victory and honour), *belongs to Allah and to His Messenger and to the believers* (upon whom He has bestowed it). (Sūra Munāfiqūn, 8)

This state of honour is the secret.

Spiritual education is not an easy matter. The material soul is in the body and is educated with it. The place of the spiritual soul is the heart. The place of the sultan-soul is the centre of the heart. The place of the holy spirit is the secret. That secret is a means of relating the truth to the believer. It is an interpreter, translating the truth to the seeker, because that secret belongs to Allah, is close to Him and is His confidant.

There are also dreams which are the result of bad character. They show the attributes of the overpowering ego or the realization of one's wrongdoings, yet one is unable to stop them.

Even in a better state, when one is reminded by Allah of one's sins and errors, one dreams of wild animals, of lions and tigers, wolves and bears, dogs and boars and smaller beasts—foxes, hares, cats, snakes, scorpions and carnivorous or poisonous, harmful animals.

To mention a few of the vices which these images represent: The tiger is the symbol of pride and egocentrism to the degree that one is arrogant to Allah Himself.

> *To those who reject Our words and turn away from them with arrogance, no opening will there be of the gates of heaven, nor will they enter the Garden until the camel can pass through the eye of the needle...* (Sūra A'rāf, 40)

The same punishment is also due to those who are arrogant to people.

The lion is a symbol of excessive love of oneself and of self-praise. The bear represents anger and rage and tyranny toward those under one's control. The wolf represents gluttony without any regard for lawfulness or unlawfulness or cleanliness or filth. The dog is the symbol of the love of this world and its troubles and its negativities. Swine are the symbol of envy, ambition, vengefulness and lust. The fox is the symbol of lying, cheating and swindling in the affairs of this world. The hare is the symbol of the same actions, except done heedlessly and unconsciously. To dream of a leopard is a sign of effort spent senselessly and irrationally, also of the desire to be prominent. The cat is a symbol of miserliness and duplicity. The snake represents lying, gossiping, making false accusations and tyrannizing people with one's words. The scorpion is the sign of negative criticism, making fun of people and rejecting them. The hornet represents subversive language that hurts people.

If one dreams of fighting with one of these beasts but not overcoming it, one needs to strengthen one's efforts, worship, and conscious remembrance, until at a stroke those animals are obliterated. If one dreams of killing these beasts, it means that one has stopped erring or causing harm to anyone. Allah mentions this: *He will remove their ills from them and improve their condition.* (Sūra Muḥammad, 2)

If one dreams of one of these animals turning into a human being it is a sign that one's previous wrong state has been turned right and that one's repentance is accepted, because the true sign of one's repentance being accepted is one's inability to do the same wrong again.

> *Accept him who repents and believes and does good deeds; for such, Allah changes their evil deeds to good ones...* (Sūra Furqān, 70)

When one is saved from wrong and evil, one must take all due care not to feel secure, for the flesh and the ego regain their strength with the slightest reminder of disobedience, revolt and vice, and cast one back to one's old ways. The state of the soul at peace can easily be lost. The reason Allah has ordered His servants to abstain from that which is unlawful is to create a continuous warning to keep one ever-vigilant.

The evil-commanding ego sometimes appears in one's dreams as a non believer; the self-criticizing self may appear as a Jew, and the inspired self sometimes appears in the form of a Christian.

CHAPTER TWENTY-THREE

On the Followers of the Mystical Path

THE people of the mystical path are divided into two sections. The first group are the Sunnīs: they follow the precepts of the Holy Qur'ān and the practices and rules derived from the behaviour and words of the Prophet ﷺ. They follow this guidance in their words, in their actions, in their thoughts and feelings, and they follow the inner meaning of the religion—that is, they understand and do not follow blindly. They act upon and live in accordance with the religious precepts, tasting them and enjoying them, not merely enduring something forced upon them. This is the mystic path which they follow. This is the brotherhood of the loving servants of Allah. Some amongst them are promised Paradise without having to give an account on the day of the Last Judgment, and others will suffer a little of the terror of the Last Day and then enter the Garden. Yet others will have to pass for a short while through hellfire to be purified of their sins before entering Paradise. None will taste the eternal fire. The eternal fire is for infidels and hypocrites.

The second group is composed of heretics. The Prophet ﷺ warned us, 'You, like the Children of Israel before you, like the community of Jesus son of Mary, will be divided and separated from each other. As they have invented and distorted, you too will create heresies. With time, in heresy, opposition and sin, you will be like them and do the same things. If they went into the lair of a poisonous reptile, you would follow them down. You should know that the Children of Israel split into seventy-one divisions. They are all in error except one. And the Christians split into seventy-two divisions, and they too are all in error except one. I fear that my people will be divided into seventy-three sections. This will be caused by their turning right into wrong and the unlawful into the lawful according to their own judgment, for their own advantage and purposes. With the exception of one, all of these divisions are Hell-bound, and that one group is saved.' When asked who the saved ones were, he answered, 'The ones who follow my beliefs and actions and those of my companions'.

The following are some of the heretical paths that call themselves mystics.

The Ḥulūliyya, Incarnationists, claim that it is lawful to look at a beautiful body or a beautiful face, whether of a woman or a man, whoever it is, whether they are wives or husbands, daughters or sisters of others. They also intermingle and dance together. This is clearly against the precepts of Islam and thc preservation of honour and decency in its laws.

There are those who are called Ḥāliyya who seek to be ecstatically entranced by singing and moving and shouting and clapping hands. They claim that their shaykhs are in such a state that they are over and above the jurisdiction of religious law. This certainly does not correspond to the behaviour of the Most Beloved of Allah, who in every way abided by religious laws.

The Awliyā'iyya claim to be in the proximity of Allah and say that when the servant comes close to Allah, all religious obligations are lifted from him. They further claim that a *walī*, the one close to Allah, becomes His friend and is therefore superior to a prophet. They say that knowledge came to the Messenger of Allah through Gabriel عليه السلام, while to the *walī* divine knowledge comes direct. Their false view of their state and what they attribute to themselves is their greatest sin, which destroys them and brings them to heresy and infidelity.

The Shamurāniyya believe that the word is eternal, and that whoever pronounces the eternal word is not bound by religious obligations; for them there is no consideration of lawful and unlawful. They use musical instruments in their rituals. They do not separate men from women. They do not see any difference between the two sexes. They are but an incorrigible gang of infidels.

The Ḥubbiyya say that when men come to the stage of love they are freed of all religious obligations. They do not conceal their private parts.

The Ḥūriyya, like the Ḥāliyya, by shouting and singing and clapping of hands seek a state of trance, and in that trance they claim to have intercourse with the houris; when they leave their trance they take total ablution. They are destroyed by their own lies.

The Ibāḥiyya refuse to propose good deeds and to forbid evil ones. On the contrary, they consider the unlawful lawful. They apply this idea to women. For them, all women are lawful to all men.

The Mutakāsiliyya make a principle out of laziness and beg from door to door for their sustenance. They claim that they are thus leaving the worldly and they rot in their laziness.

The Mutajāhiliyya feign ignorance and purposely dress immodestly, trying to look and behave like nonbelievers, while Allah says *Do not incline towards the wrongdoers...* (Sūra Hūd, 113) And the Prophet ﷺ says, 'Whoever tries to appear like a people is considered to be one of them'.

The Wāfiqiyya claim that only Allah is able to know Allah. Therefore they abandon the path of seeking truth, and their purposeful ignorance leads them to destruction.

The Ilhāmiyya count on inspiration, abandon knowledge, forbid study, and say that the Qur'ān is a veil for them and that the poetic muse is their Qur'ān. They abandon the Qur'ān and prayers and teach their children poetry instead.

The leaders and teachers of the Sunnī path say that the Companions, with the blessing of the words and presence of the Prophet ﷺ, were in a high state of spiritual ecstasy and rapture. In later times this spiritual level dissipated. It passed to the spiritual inheritors of the divine path to truth, which in turn divided into many branches. It was divided into so many sections that the wisdom and the energy thinned and dispersed. In many cases all that was left was only an appearance wrapped in the clothing of a spiritual teacher without any meaning beneath it. Even in that empty state it kept multiplying and dividing, turning into heresy. Some became Qalandarī—wandering beggars. Others became Ḥaydarī and pretended to be heroes. Still others called themselves Adhamī and pretended to follow Ḥaḍrat Ibrāhīm Adham's abandonment of the sultanate of this world. There are so many more.

In our time, those who follow the path of truth in accordance with the religious law are fewer than few. The true followers of this path are known by two witnesses. One is the exterior witness, which shows that the seeker's daily life is reinforced by religious ordinances and practices. The second, the inner witness, is the example the seeker follows and emulates and by which he is guided. Indeed, there is none other to follow than the Prophet of Allah ﷺ, who is the means, the bridge, and at one time the seeker and the truth he seeks. Without doubt his divine spirit is the only intermediary. That is the law which must be followed for the continuation of religious order in the life of a real believer. Alternatively a saintly being who embodies the inheritance of the Prophet's spirituality may bless the seeker with his material presence. Indeed, the Devil cannot assume the shape of our Prophet ﷺ.

Beware, O traveller on the path to truth, that the blind do not lead the blind. Your sight should be so keen that you are able to distinguish the smallest particle of good from the smallest particle of evil.

CHAPTER TWENTY-FOUR

Afterword

THE traveller on the path to truth must have intelligence, understanding and insight. These are his prerequisites.

Allah created servants wise and understanding
Who leave the world, the abode of afflictions.
They take to the sea where waves are their only trial,
Where good deeds are ships on which to ride the waves.

The traveller is on the path because there is a place to which he wishes to go. His attention is fixed principally upon that goal, yet he cannot ignore the importance of the preparation for this voyage. When he prepares he must take heed not to be fooled by the attraction of appearances, and he must not load himself with luggage nor take the stops and stations as his final goal.

The people of the mystic path say that deeds belong to the One who created them. Man is not fully responsible: in his hands deeds may appear other than what they are. Allah says

. . . none is secure from Allah's scheme except the people who have lost everything [and are in total want]. (Sūra Aʿrāf, 99)

This is fundamental on this path: to leave all luggage behind and depend on Allah, undistracted by the temptations of the stations on the path. In a divine tradition Allah says:

O Muḥammad, give the good news to the sinners that I am All-Forgiving. But tell the ones who are truly Mine and sincere in their wish for Me that I am Most Jealous (of anything that they may wish for besides Me).

The miracles that appear through those close to God and the spiritual stations in which they appear are true. Yet even such people are not safe from Allah's schemes and His tests inciting them to sin—sometimes they are even granted Success when they begin to sin, so they may think that their states belong to them and that the miracles are theirs. It is only the prophets and their miracles that are free from such tests. It is said that the fear of losing one's faith at one's last breath is the only safeguard that will grant faith at one's last moment.

Ḥaḍrat Ḥasan al-Baṣrī, may Allah sanctify his secret, used to say that the ones close to Allah succeed through their fear of Allah. In them, fear well exceeds hope because they know the danger of being fooled by human nature. These delusions drive one out of the path without one even knowing it. He also said that the healthy person fears sickness and his hopes are few, while the sick person no longer fears falling sick, and his hope for health grows.

The Prophet ﷺ says, 'If one weighed the fear and the hope of the faithful, one would find them equal'. By Allah's grace, at our last breath, Allah increases our hope over our fear. In the words of our Prophet ﷺ, 'All my people will take their last breaths with trust and hope in Allah's mercy'. For Allah promises: *My mercy encompasses all things...* (Sūra A'rāf, 156) and, 'My mercy far surpasses My wrath'.

Allah is the Most Compassionate and the Most Merciful of the Merciful, and one may certainly depend on that. Yet the traveller on the path of truth must fear and escape from Allah's wrath. For this it is necessary that he present to Him all that he possesses—his very being, his existence—place everything at His feet and take refuge from Him in Him.

O seeker, fall on your knees in front of your Lord! Strip yourself of your material being! Confess and repent for your past errors and wait at the gate of his mercy without anything, in complete want! If you do this, you will certainly receive His grace, His blessings, His enlightenment, His love and compassion; and all your sins and impurities will melt away from you. For He is the Beneficent, the Most Compassionate and Generous, the Eternal Lord, the All-powerful.

We beg for peace and blessings upon our Master the Prophet and his progeny, companions and followers. All grace and thanks belong to Allah; we leave all in His hands.

AMĪN